SAINT THÉRÈSE
THE LITTLE FLOWER

The Making of a Saint

*And we know that to them that love God,
all things work together unto good,
to such as, according to* his *purpose,
are called* to be *saints.*

Romans 8:28

*More than ever I realize that the smallest
happenings of our life are guided by God.*

St. Thérèse of the Child Jesus
November, 1896

TAN BOOKS AND PUBLISHERS, INC.
Rockford, Illinois 61105

About The Author

John Beevers was born in 1912 in Yorkshire, England. He attended Cambridge University, starting in 1929, where he took a "double first" in the English Tripos. In the early 30's he began a journalist career with the *Manchester Daily Dispatch*. In 1934 he was appointed literary editor of the *Sunday Referee*. Just before World War II he joined the *Daily Express* as an assistant lead writer, and shortly thereafter became editorial assistant in the Ministry of Information.

Bad health excluded him from military service during the War, so he joined the B.B.C. in 1941, where he remained until 1969, rising to executive status. He preferred, however, to remain in the journalistic area rather than enter the administrative.

In the 1950's he started writing books in his spare time, eventually having published fifteen—mostly saintly biographies, but also some translations of spiritual works from the French. His *Storm of Glory* (1950) cast a new light on St. Thérèse of Lisieux. A few years later he rendered a new translation of her autobiography, *The Story of a Soul,* which is still in print and selling well.

Recently, Mr. Beevers translated and had published Father de Caussade's *Abandonment to Divine Providence.* The present book was finished in 1972 and was originally to have appeared in 1973, during the centenary (1873-1973) of St. Thérèse's birth.

Mr. Beevers passed away September 13, 1975, leaving a widow, a daughter (in Seattle), and two grandchildren. The *Psalms* tell us "Precious in the sight of the Lord is the death of his saints." (115). Precious to the Lord also must be the life and death of one who has made better known the lives and achievements of His heroes. *Requiescat in pace.*

7

Chapter 1

INTRODUCTION

A saint is not a freak. He is, as we all are, a being born with a normal share of human frailties and burdened with hereditary flaws and powers such as afflict and strengthen all the sons and daughters of Adam. He has not escaped the stain of Original Sin. And as he passes from infancy, through adolescence, to maturity, he, too, is subject to the multitude of influences that press upon us all, and he has our own same freedom to accept or reject them.

Therefore, when we study a saint, we cannot know him fully unless we know what these influences were, how he was tugged this way and that, who his parents and teachers were, the effect on him of his brothers and sisters, his friends and his acquaintances. We know, of course, that it is the grace of God which makes a saint. But we are left free to co-operate with that grace or to turn aside from it. The choice is ours. In this matter, God waives His omnipotence. He persuades. He does not compel. And often, as the stories of the saints repeatedly show, He does not always choose to act directly upon the soul. He sometimes prefers to use agents, to allow His creatures to act for Him in the work of making a saint.

So it was with the great saint of modern times, St. Thérèse of the Child Jesus. Sanctity has its mysteries which we shall never understand in this life, and it is foolish presumption to pretend we can fully explain it, either its genesis, its development, or its full flowering. We can describe, but we cannot penetrate into its fiery depths. Even the great mystical saints stammer or fail when they try to tell what they know. Yet it is only the very core of saintliness which resists all our probings, but there is much that we can understand and profitably discuss.

I have already written about St. Thérèse,* but since then much new material about her family has appeared, and we have, for the first time, the complete text of her autobiography as she wrote it. With every fresh disclosure it becomes more and more apparent that God used her family and later the community of nuns she entered as His instruments in fashioning her into a saint. She was not born with the halo of sanctity already in position. As a saint she was—always under God, it must be understood—created by her family and her fellow nuns. Today the family is no longer the key unite of civilization. Over too much of the world, the state is supreme and overrides both the natural and the supernatural rights of the family. In her person and in her teaching, St. Thérèse offers us both an example and a body of precepts which are invaluable. A knowledge and understanding of her environment, which, given her total response to grace, made her sanctity inevitable, are of equal value. That is what I attempt to offer here.

Storm of Glory (New York: Sheed and Ward). 1950.

Chapter 2

FAMILY BACKGROUND

The roll of saints includes kings and beggars, men and women of all degrees, some with a lineage as long as their arm, others unable to name their grandparents. The family of St. Thérèse—her immediate ancestors—were not distinguished by rank, wealth or intellect, nor were they anonymous peasants, living from hand to mouth without a penny to call their own. They were people who had a small, but honorable and well-defined position in the state. Her paternal grandfather, Pierre François Martin, was born in 1777 in Normandy. When he was twenty-two, he joined the army and made soldiering his profession for the next thirty-one years. He followed Napoleon's eagles through Prussia and Poland and fought for him in France when the Emperor's days of power were numbered. He won promotion and, after the restoration of the Bourbons, reached the rank of captain.

At the age of forty-one, he married the eighteen-year old daughter of another army captain, also a veteran of the Grande Armée. They had five children. The third was Louis Joseph Aloys Stanislas Martin, who was to be the father of St. Thérèse. He was born in Bordeaux on August 22, 1823, and until he was seven and his father retired, the family moved from one garrison town to another, finally ending up in Strasbourg. On his retirement, Captain Pierre decided to spend the rest of his life in his native Normandy and chose Alençon for his home, a quiet little grey-stone town with the river Sarthe meandering through it.

There he became a well-known figure as, tall and straight as a ramrod, he walked through the streets in his

working on the delicate and intricate machinery of a watch, was a task most suitable for him.

In the autumn of 1843, he left Brittany to go to Strasbourg, breaking his journey with a brief holiday in Switzerland where he visited the monastery of the Great St. Bernard, high in the Alps. Louis stayed two years in Strasbourg where, apart from mastering the final mysteries of his craft, he learned German and, with the son of his father's friend, made long trips through the countryside of Alsace. They both loved swimming, and on one occasion, Louis nearly lost his own life in saving that of his friend.

He was just twenty-two when he made an attempt to abandon the world for the cloister. In September, 1845, he left Strasbourg to pay a second visit to the monastery of the Great St. Bernard, this time, however, not as a tourist but as a would-be postulant. The prior received him kindly, but when he questioned him about his education and found that he knew no Latin, he declared that it would be impossible to admit him without a fair working knowledge of the language of the Church and advised him to return home and acquire it.

Back in Alençon, Louis confided in his parish priest, who told him how to set about the task. So grammars and textbooks were bought, and he paid a tutor for a hundred and twenty lessons. But it all came to nothing, and by the beginning of 1847 his studies were abandoned. Louis Martin was an able mechanic and shrewd businessman, but he was quite without any academic talent. Providentially so, for had he been able to master Cicero's way with the subjunctive and the ablative absolute, the Augustinian canons would have gained a monk and the world have lost a saint.

After this failure, he went to Paris and stayed there nearly three years. Towards the end of 1850, he was back in Alençon where he acquired a large house and shop in a quiet part of town, setting up as a jeweler as well as a watchmaker. His parents came to live with him and there, for nearly nine years, he led a hard-working and almost solitary life. When he was not attending to his business, he took long walks deep into the countryside or, more often, exercised his skill as a fisherman, which was considerable. (He was also a fair shot.) Most of the fish he caught were given to the convent of Poor Clares in the town.

The desire for solitude grew upon him and, after some years, he bought a small property on the edge of Alençon. Known as the Pavilion, it was a six-sided, three-storied tower with a room on each floor. It stood in a secluded garden, and there Louis used to withdraw to read and meditate. It was sparsely furnished: a table and a chair or two in the ground-floor room, a few books, and on the wall a crucifix and sentences painted there by Louis: "God sees me." "Eternity draws near and we don't give it a thought." "Blessed are they who keep the law of the Lord." It stands today, almost unchanged.

The one thing he had no thought of was marriage, yet less than fifteen months after his purchase of the Pavilion he was a married man with Zélie Guérin as his wife.

Zélie's childhood was not a happy one. She herself said her mother was too severe and that her youth had been as gloomy as a funeral. Mrs. Guérin, though a pious woman, seemed to lack all knowledge of how to handle children. She never, for example, allowed Zélie to have a doll, and she inflicted on the household an austerity which was Puritan rather than Catholic, yet she pampered and spoiled her son, probably because he was born ten years after Zélie, long after she had ceased to hope for a boy. Zélie and her sister went to school at the Convent of the Perpetual Adoration in Alençon; their parents had moved to the town in 1844. She was a good pupil, bright and hard-working.

Like her future husband, she wished to enter religion, and again like him, she was turned away. Her desire was to become a Sister of St. Vincent de Paul, and it would seem that she had every qualification: she was deeply religious, energetic and tireless, and overflowing with com-

there, and see to it that she married well. But Zélie thanked her, smiled and refused to go.

Yet within three months of their chance enounter on the bridge, she and Louis were married—just after midnight on July 13, 1858. The place was the church of Notre-Dame in Alençon; the time is strange to us, but in the France of their day it was not unusual. Far more unusual was the fact that, on the morning after her midnight wedding, Zélie caught the early train to Le Mans and saw her sister in the Visitation Convent. And there she wept. Nearly twenty years later she vividly remembered her emotion and could say that she wept more than she had ever done before or was ever to do again. "That day I shed all my tears" are the words she uses. She saw her sister where she herself longed to be and realized that now the conventual life could never be hers. She felt she had lost a great treasure and she sobbed her heart out. What went on in Louis' mind at this tearful start to his married life we do not know, though Zélie says: "He understood and did his best to comfort me."

Zélie was quite ignorant of the so-called "facts of life," so she may not have known what her husband was talking about when he suggested that they should live together as brother and sister. She, of course, left her parents and set up her lace-making business in Louis' house. His parents occupied one floor and the newly-married couple had the rest of the house to themselves. As her wedding-portion, Zélie had brought with her two thousand five hundred dollars; Louis' capital was nearly twice that and, besides cash, he owned his house and shop and the Pavilion. Both their businesses were thriving, so they were comfortably off.

For ten months they lived a life in which sex played no part. They must, however, have wanted children from the very first, for they adopted a small boy. It was not a legal adoption. It seems that they offered to look after the boy and that his parents—who presumably had a large family—were willing to let him go. The words "seems" and presumably" have to be used, for hardly anything is known about the episode. But in less than a year the boy was back with his family, for a priest—the Martin's confessor—had told them both that they should behave as married couples were meant to behave and have children of their own.

The start of this married life makes a curious story, and it is one that has driven several writers dealing with St. Thérèse to perform extraordinary feats of verbal and spiritual legerdemain in efforts to prove how admirable was the behavior of Mr. and Mrs. Martin. It has even been said that God, whose Son was born of a Virgin, would entrust St. Thérèse only to parents who had shown themselves able to grasp—because they had practiced it—the full splendor of virginity in the married state. This is offensive nonsense, a statement which shows a total lack of comprehension of what Christian marriage is.

We can never know with certainty what caused Louis and Zélie to begin their life together so unnaturally, nor if it were only the words of their confessor which brought them to normality. One can speculate, though, and I would say that, when young, they both mistook ther vocation, which, as the future was to show, was for marriage. But for some years, as we have seen, they hankered after the religious life. Very probably, too, they were neither of them highly sexed. Louis, however, was continually badgered by his mother to get married and, knowing the joy that Zélie felt when she did have children, it is hard to imagine that she felt no physical longing for them as she sat, a single woman, working at her lace.

The inevitable propinquity of marriage must also have played its part. Their confessor's advice may have been advice they were only too glad to accept. For, at the baptism of their first child, Mr. Martin told the priest: "It's the first time you've seen me at a baptism, but I assure you that it won't be the last." After all her children were born, Mrs. Martin told how much they meant to her and Louis. She declared that, when the children began coming, their yearning for a life in religion weakened.

They lived only for their children and found all their happiness in them.

In the years immediately before their marriage it would, I think, have been hard to imagine a couple apparently more unsuitable for marriage and parenthood, both longing to withdraw from the world, both immersed in work and their religious duties, and neither of them ever showing any interest in the opposite sex. Yet they were chosen to be the parents of a great saint and to present to the world a picture of a truly Christian family. Their story is an impressive manifestation of the power of God to fashion the most unlikely material into perfect instruments to serve His purpose.

Their case is also a justification of Christian marriage, not that such a marriage should have to be justified. Unhappily, however, marriage is a state of life which is constantly under attack and never more so than in this century. "Openly and without any sense of shame, people treat the sanctity of marriage with derision and contempt. The spoken and the written word, theatrical performances of every kind, novels, love stories, humorous tales, films and broadcasts—all the latest inventions of modern science—are used to this end. And these ideas are being instilled into every category of mankind—rich and poor, workers and employers, learned and unlearned, single and married, believers and unbelievers, young and old." These are the words of Pius XI and, since he wrote them more than forty years ago, they have acquired still greater force and urgency.

The words of St. Paul are largely forgotten: "Marriage, in every way, must be held in honor." Today, the idea of indissoluble marriage, of marriage as a true Sacrament is held by many to be intellectually contemptible; marriage is convenient and, when it becomes inconvenient, it can and should be ended. This is the attitude of much of the Western world.

It is a little different under Communism. There, in recent years, marriage has been treated with increasing seriousness and with none of the frivolity too prevalent in Scandinavia, in England, and in the United States. This is a good thing, and yet behind the Communist attitude there is a grievous error. Moscow approves stable marriages, seeing them as a major asset to the State—which indeed they are—but a cardinal tenet of Marxism is that the family, which is the product and the main purpose of marriage, is subordinate to and negligible alongside the State. The family exists for the State; whereas, in reality, the State came into being solely to protect the family and the individual, and that should still be its chief purpose. No Communist would ever recognize the truth that "human beings are born primarily for heaven and eternity, not for earth and time."

In the Martin family we are shown what a marriage can and should be. Though it resulted in the birth of a girl who was to become a great saint, that is something which, in one sense, is irrelevant. The marriage of Louis and Zélie and the family life it generated would have been no less a noble example had there been no Thérèse, but her existence has focused attention on them. Without her, they would have lived and died unknown.

That is not the point of her sanctity: it has a far greater purpose than to illuminate her family. Yet a side effect of it is to turn a searchlight onto this devout, obscure circle so that we, more than a century away, can see that it is a possible and a splendid thing to live as its members did—not literally, of course, in their day-to-day manner, for they were compelled as we all are to make adjustments to the circumstances of their own time and place—but to live conscious always of the presence of God and to be determined to make glad obedience to His will the sole guide in dealing with the multifarious events of life.

Chapter 3

THE MARTINS—ZELIE

The first four children of the Martins were girls: Marie-Louise, Marie-Pauline, Marie-Léonie and Marie-Hélène. They came quickly—between February, 1860, and October, 1864. Two boys followed: Marie-Joseph-Louis and Marie-Joseph-Jean-Baptiste. It was Mrs. Martin's dearest wish to give the Church a missionary priest, and the birth of her first son gave her intense delight.

A few days after his birth she was saying what a splendid figure he would present as he celebrated Mass, and she began to think about making him a chasuble of Alençon lace for the day of his ordination. But he lived for less than six months. He was the first of four of their children who were to die in infancy. After her first three children, Mrs. Martin was unable to feed the others, and they were all sent out to nurse. Whether or not this harmed them we do not know, but from what can be gathered from Mrs. Martin's descriptions of the illnesses of those who died, it seems that there was nothing constitutionally wrong with them, and that they were lost because of the primitive medicine and hygiene in a small town of the 1860's.

The second, Joseph, died when he was nine months old. In the spring of 1869 a seventh child was born, Marie-Céline. She was to survive. But early in the following year Marie-Hélène, then just turned five, fell ill with what seemed to be a feverish cold. The doctor found nothing seriously wrong with her. A day or two later he said she was gravely ill with congestion of the lungs, and later that morning she died in her mother's arms.

Mrs. Martin felt this loss far more sharply than she did

that of her two boys, for Hélène had grown into an attractive little girl, intelligent and good, a little girl liked by everyone and easily her father's favorite. Years after her death he would, deeply moved, recite the lines of Chateaubriand which begin: "Ah! Who will restore my Hélène to me?"

Thus, in ten years, the Martins lost four of their children, and the fathers of both Louis and of Zélie also died. It is a melancholy catalogue and one that makes it evident that this was not a family spared the sufferings common to us all. In addition to this succession of bereavements, Mrs. Martin, in the spring of 1865, had the first warnings of the cancer of the breast that was to kill her. She wrote to tell her brother of it, saying that she was never without some discomfort in her breast. It was a discomfort that was to grow into a savage pain and be her companion for the next twelve years.

The Martins were not stoics in the face of death and suffering. They wept when their children died. Zélie was shocked at the physical aspect of death. When she saw the cold, still face of her dead father-in-law, she was appalled to think that she might see her children looking the same or that they might see her frozen in the terrible immobility of the dead. Yet their natural grief was never inordinate. They knew that all things are ordered by God, and as Zélie exclaimed in her sorrow, God is a good Father who never burdens His children with more than they can carry. Her sister, the Visitation nun, told her: "One day your unshakable trust in God will be splendidly recompensed. You can be very sure that He will bless you . . . wouldn't you feel you had a rich reward if God, so well pleased with you, gave you a child who would become that great saint you have so longed for?" These words were written three years before the birth of Thérèse.

So far, all their children had been born in the house attached to Mr. Martin's shop, but in 1871 a move was made to the house which had belonged to Zélie's father. It stands in the Rue Saint-Blaise, opposite the Prefecture,

Now the Martins undoubtedly lived an enclosed life. It is true that one day a week Mrs. Martin saw all the girls who were making lace for her, that Mr. Martin made frequent business trips, that he went fishing, that the two eldest girls—Marie and Pauline—were sent away from home to be boarders at the school run by the Visitation nuns at Le Mans, that there were visits to Lisieux and, of course, attendance at Mass every morning. But there was rarely any attempt to mingle with their neighbors. Neither Mr. nor Mrs. Martin had what is normally understood as a friend. A few acquaintances, yes, and Mr. Martin knew one or two priests. Yet—and it is astonishing—when we examine the family life of the Martins, we get no sense of claustrophobia; instead, there is about it a feeling of life, bustle and merriment, and, running steadily underneath, a current of profound and unquenchable joy.

Today the family as it should be has almost disappeared. Grandparents and elderly parents are left to fend for themselves. Bare, cold single rooms in the great cities of the West are inhabited by lonely old people whose children can no longer be bothered with them. And where is the firm yet loving concern under which children used to be reared? The family is a divine institution, the basic unit of civilization, yet now it is more a legal term than a reality. What a family should be can be known by considering the Martins. That is not to say that their family life should be copied in every detail. They lived in a particular time and in a particular country. Their circumstances are not ours, and no slavish imitation of their activities would help us. But their attitude to the family, their bearing of one another's burdens, their sense of responsibility, their eagerness to ensure that every member was helped, loved, or reproved—as need arose—none of this is outdated. Such principles are always and universally valid.

The first thing to note about the Martin family is that the loving service of God was its prime concern.

Nothing else mattered. Mr. and Mrs. Martin heard Mass every morning, and as they grew old enough, their children went with them. When he retired from business, Mr. Martin visited the Blessed Sacrament every afternoon. From time to time he made a retreat, and he went on frequent pilgrimages, sometimes to a nearby shrine, sometimes as far as Chartres.

There was a good deal of anti-clerical feeling in Alençon, and Mr. Martin always went out of his way to manifest his devotion to the Church. When a crowd of pilgrims arrived back in the town from Lourdes, there was waiting for them at the station, a hostile gathering which greeted them with jeers and catcalls. Mr. Martin was there. He threw a large wooden rosary round his neck, put himself at the head of the pilgrims and led the way through the crowd. Taking part on one occasion in a procession of the Blessed Sacrament, he stepped out of its ranks for a second to knock off the hat of a spectator who, with open mockery, refused to bare his head as the monstrance passed him.

He went even beyond the advice of a priest in his determination to keep Sunday holy and to perform no servile work on that day. This priest suggested to him that he would be doing no wrong if he opened his shop for an hour or two on Sunday morning, for it was then that many people flocked into the town from the neighboring villages. Many shops opened and did a thriving trade, but Mr. Martin would have none of it. Years later one of his daughters said: "The chief virtues I saw practiced at home were the keeping of Sunday holy and contempt for the world."

Mr. Martin obeyed strictly the fasts and abstinences ordered by the Church—sometimes to his wife's embarrassment. When a relative from Paris suggested coming to visit them, Mrs. Martin wrote in some agitation to her brother and urged him to persuade the lady to put back her visit for a week because if she came during the week she had planned, her stay might coincide with three Ember Days and Louis would eat no meat then and would·

the little girl's soul a sense, a feeling of purity of such sweetness that no words could express. Pauline notes laconically: "It was a Saturday and it was not a dream."

Thérèse saw Our Lady smile, but with all her mother's down-to-earth matter-of-factness, she was never sentimental about the Mother of God. She never pictured her in the semblance of those terrible, unreal figures which are the shame of too many Catholic churches. When she herself was near death, she said she knew that Our Lady was not free from the ills of the flesh during her life on earth. She suffered from the heat and the cold, and she was often tired and hungry. Thérèse saw her as a young and poor Jewish mother who knew all the tribulations of family life; she was not an ethereal figure who lived in the world yet was insulated from its harshness.

Her love for the Blessed Virgin began early. Céline has said: "Thérèse was not four when she showed how pleased she was to say her prayers before Our Lady's altar. She clapped her hands and jumped up and down with delight when she saw it decked with flowers. When she was older, she loved to decorate the altar we had at home with lights and flowers." This is Céline talking when the greatness of Thérèse was beginning to be widely known, and we must allow for that in considering her words. We must also realize that an untutored aborigine would take pleasure in an ornate altar. But that said, we know that Thérèse was precocious in spiritual matters and that it is more than likely that she realized, in a childlike way, the importance of Our Lady.

A nun, who was a novice with Thérèse, testifies; "I was always very impressed with the great love she had for the Blessed Virgin. Once she got talking about her, she could go on forever." During the whole of her life in Carmel, she never began any task without a swift appeal to Our Lady, and when Pauline, then her prioress, ordered her to write the story of her life, she went away and knelt before the statue of the Blessed Virgin—the one which had smiled on her and healed her—and begged her to guide her pen so that she would not write a line displeasing to her.

She always had the right word to say to the novices when she was acting as novice-mistress. They were often astonished at the manner in which she put her finger unerringly on their problems, and they questioned her, asking how she managed to do it. She answered at once: "I never begin talking to you without having first prayed to the Blessed Virgin and asked her to tell me what to say to you which will do you most good. I'm often astonished myself at what I tell you, but I feel I never made a mistake, for it is Jesus who is speaking through me."

She told one nun: "I like to hide all my troubles from God, for I want to appear always happy before Him, but I hide nothing from the Blessed Virgin, and I tell her everything." The very last words that Thérèse wrote, in fact, were addressed to Our Lady. In this one short sentence is the distillation of all her love: "Oh Mary, if I were the Queen of Heaven and you were Thérèse, I should want to be Thérèse so that you might be the Queen of Heaven."

Mrs. Martin was a charitable woman. Take, for example, her relationship with her servants. She declared as a general principle that all servants should always feel that their employer is really fond of them. They must always be treated with sympathetic kindness, and there must never be anything stiff and unbending in one's attitude to them. She admitted that she herself was inclined to be rather brisk and sharp in manner, and yet she was adored by all the servants she ever had, and they stayed with her as long as she needed them. For, as she said: "I treat my servants just as I do my own children." If one fell ill, she nursed her herself, sometimes sitting up through the night. Years after her death, Louise, her former housemaid, said: "For Mrs. Martin anything was good enough, but for anyone else nothing was too good." Should any of the girls she employed in lace-making fall ill, she at once visited them, taking little gifts and comforting them with sympathy and prayer.

In all her dealings with her servants she remembered the words of St. Paul: "Masters, do to your servants that which is just and equal: knowing that you also have a master in heaven." Today, charity such as that shown by Mrs. Martin angers all who flaunt the title of progressives, as it smacks too much of those Victorian days when, in rural England, the lady of the manor and her daughters took bread and soup and nourishing jellies to the squalid cottages of the "laboring poor." Today, also, if one is sufficiently well-off to be able to employ servants, they will not stay for very long unless they are treated rather better than one's children.

Matters were very different in the middle of last century, and it is in the light of the situation which prevailed then that we must judge the quality of Mrs. Martin's charity. Servants were too often overworked and underpaid, and they were liable to instant dismissal at the whim of their employer. A man could fall ill, lose his job and quickly starve. If you were old, penniless and alone in the world, your prospects were bleak, for murderers in their jails are far better cared for now than were the nineteenth-century aged in their workhouses. Public charity was mean and grudging. It had the air of a punishment society was inflicting upon its failures, and without private benevolence, the lot of the unfortunate would have been insupportable.

Mrs. Martin could do little, but what she could do she did, eagerly and cheerfully, and those who received her charity were grateful. Strangers were relieved as readily as those of her immediate circle. She was walking in the countryside one day when she passed a ragged old man. Giving Thérèse some money, she told her to offer it to him. He appeared to so grateful that she asked him to come home with them. There she gave him a good dinner and a pair of boots. His story was a pitiful one. He had no home and slept in a deserted, tumbledown hut. From time to time, someone took pity on him and gave him a copper or two. For food, he was reduced to hanging around the town's barracks and begging for scraps. Mrs. Martin told him he was free to come to her whenever he wanted, and she would always give him food. Before long, Mr. Martin succeeded in getting him into a home for the aged—not an institution of any great luxury, one can be sure, but one where he would, at least, neither freeze nor starve, as he had done the previous winter.

Enemies of her country were not excluded from her charity. Nine German soldiers were billeted on the Martins during the Franco-Prussian war of 1870. One of them, little more than a lad, was miserable with homesickness. Zélie went out of her way to be kind to him, chatting and joking with him and secretly giving him special little dishes of food.

She was a bustling, cheerful woman, but she was without illusions about the world, eagerly doing her duty in it, but always insisting that we must not expect the world to give us great and lasting joy. They who did cherish this expectation were wrong, and their hopes always rudely shattered. True happiness was not to be found in this life: God had ordered it thus so that we should never forget that our true home was elsewhere. Throughout her letters, there is a steady insistence on the transience of life and on the fact that we may die at any moment.

She had little use for what she called "the brief pleasures of earth" and she was quick to seize on any happening which illustrated the folly of trusting in such pleasures. She knew a young married couple who were rich and happy. One night they went to spend an evening at a local café with some relatives. At about half-past eight, the husband remembered he had a letter to post. His wife went with him. They took a short cut through their garden, but forgot there was a trench at the bottom. They fell into it and were both killed. Writing to tell her brother of this, Zélie declared that the young wife used to exult in her happiness: "I want for nothing . . . I am rich and healthy . . . I can have anything I want . . . no one could be happier." And she warned him that disaster lies in wait for those who rejoice too greatly in possessing the good things in life.

Thérèse, truly her daughter in this as in so many other attitudes, wrote to Céline: "What do earthly things matter to us? Oh! What effort it takes to go on living and to stay amidst the bitterness and anguish of life on earth." And to Pauline: "If only you knew how much I wish to be indifferent to worldy things. What does the beauty of created things matter to me? Even if I owned them all, I should be very unhappy, for my heart would remain so empty." Also, when Marie, her eldest sister, was upset at the dispersal of the furniture of their home in Lisieux during the fatal illness of their father, Thérèse told her that life would pass very quickly and that, when they were in heaven, the fate of this furniture could not possibly interest them.

Thérèse never felt at home in this life. As a young schoolgirl she loved Sundays, but as each Sunday drew to its close melancholy invaded her spirit. She thought of the next day when the ordinary, everyday round of work and lessons would begin again: "I felt that I was an exile on earth and I longed for the eternal peace of Heaven, the never-ending Sabbath of our true Fatherland."

Pauline, too, shared this outlook of her mother. When she was the prioress of the Lisieux Carmel, she told a nun who was ill that it was no use her thinking that, once her suffering was over, she could look forward to a spell of well-being and happiness: "No, no! That is only certain in heaven. Down here tribulation follows tribulation, but one day, by the grace of God, we shall find ourselves beneath a sky that is always blue." She declared that both the tribulations and the glories of the world would vanish like a flash of lightning, but that a life of holiness had no end. The night of death was the gateway to eternal day.

Mrs. Martin not only spoke in general terms of the evanescence of worldly delights; she kept herself very firmly from any involvement in them. In Alençon there was a woman—we know her only as Mrs. X.—who was a close acquaintance of Mrs. Martin. In a letter to Pauline,

Mrs. Martin said she knew that this woman, despite her great fortune, was not happy. She had one of the most splendid houses in the town, with huge and richly furnished rooms. But what was the use of it all? No one visited her there except the very people she did not want to see, as she considered them her inferiors by birth. She realized that her daughter was growing up in such isolation that she had been forced to give frequent evening parties for young girls of a similar age. Marie went to them, but Mrs. Martin was a little uneasy, for she knew that to mix with the very rich can quickly give rise to envious longings.

And Marie was at times a little dazzled by the luxury she saw in some of the homes she visited. She longed for her own family to move into a house in one of the fashionable and expensive streets of the town, once spending a whole afternoon trying to persuade her mother to take this step by saying how much she wanted to live in a spacious, beautiful, and well-furnished room.

But before long, Mrs. Martin was able to declare that she was very happy about the way Marie was changing. Worldly matters no longer made as much impression on her as did things of the spirit. True, she still had a long way to go before entering fully on the road to perfection, but she was moving steadily towards it. Mrs. Martin always insisted that she had no desire to associate with the rich and fashionable, but always honest about her feelings, she once said that she thought it was pride which kept her away from them, for she could not, as we should say, keep up with them: "It would cost me too much. I should be likely to waste both time and money." Yet she could write to her sister-in-law to tell her—with pleasure—that Marie, along with several other young girls, was going to spend a fortnight with Mrs. X.

Marie had mentioned this trip to Pauline and Pauline had passed on the news to the Visitation nun who was her aunt and Mrs. Martin's sister. And, said Mrs. Martin, her sister was displeased at Marie's holiday. Indignantly she asked: "Are we supposed to shut ourselves up in a convent? When living in the world one cannot behave like a savage. Besides, I quite like the idea of Marie having some entertainment. It will help to cure her of her shyness. One mustn't accept everything my sister says, saintly woman though she is."

It was, one sees, possible for Mrs. Martin to be inconsistent and to be a very human mother, unwilling to take advice from anyone about the handling of her own children.

However, it is certain that Mr. and Mrs. Martin's rejection of much of life, their insistence on the vanity of all earthly things, deeply affected the Martin children. We have noted how completely Thérèse wished to disassociate herself from the world. Céline, too, was never happy in it. During the last years of her father's life, when he was both physically paralyzed and mentally deranged, she used to take him to spend the summer months with her aunt and uncle and cousins at the chateau of La Musse, a very handsome property which her uncle had inherited. The house, a large one, stood in a park of nearly a hundred acres dotted with clumps of magnificent trees. They were very comfortable months, packed with parties, pleasure trips, and the quiet entertaining of friends. But Céline was unhappy. She disliked having servants waiting on her and, every now and then, she felt suffocated by the luxury surrounding her.

Once, when driving out on a visit, she suddenly realized she was lolling back among the cushions of the carriage. No very great fault, one would have imagined, but this moment of ease filled her with self-contempt. "Can this really be me taking part in this farce?" And she ripped off her wrist a bracelet she had just bought. "And here I'm wearing this chain. Am I a slave?"

When Pauline was a boarder at the Visitation Convent at Le Mans, she found that nearly all the other pupils were of "noble" birth: in other words, at some time or another their ancestors had acquired the right to insert "de" in their name. Recalling her school days, Pauline spoke of the unbelievable vanity of these girls. One pestered her to find out if she had not at least one aristocrat in her family. Pauline fortunately remembered a Monsieur de Lacauve, a cousin of her father. This girl then went on to ask her what was the color of the drawing room at home and the color, too, of its sofa. Pauline had not the courage to admit that her home had no drawing room, but she suddenly recalled that at the Pavilion, Mr. Martin's little retreat, there was a wickerwork chair, yellow in color. So she hastily told her questioner that the drawing room sofa was yellow. "Most distinguished" was the comment. "Vanity of vanities!" exclaims Pauline, a severe and humorless judgment on a most harmless scrap of schoolgirl chatter.

Mrs. Martin's behavior in the face of death—her own—discloses a great deal about her. It throws into high relief the complete absence of sentimentality in her character, her almost brutal realism, her courage and her cheerful submission to the will of God. It was in 1865 that she began to be troubled by a swelling in her breast. Nothing was done about it and it was quiescent for many years, but in 1876 the swelling developed and reluctantly, but driven by the anxiety of her husband and brother, she visited a doctor. She had no great opinion of doctors. A hundred years ago, they did not receive the absurd adulation that they enjoy today.

This particular doctor she did not like as a person, but he was a man after her own heart in one respect: he minced no words and gave her the truth instead of soothing syrup. After a thorough examination, he told her she had cancer. Did she reject the thought of an operation? She declared that she did not, but she felt sure that it would shorten her life rather than save it. He agreed that an operation would almost certainly be useless, but offered to prescribe some medicine. "What good would that do?" she asked. He looked her full in the face: "None at all, but it would reassure some patients."

She told him she was grateful for his frankness as it gave her time to put her affairs in order so that they would be no trouble to her family after her death. Some three months before she died she declared that this consultation had been of priceless value to her. When it was over, she hurried home and repeated the doctor's words. Everyone burst into tears but, by talking of people who had lived ten or fifteen years after such a medical verdict and by discussing the matter in her usual tone of quiet cheerfulness, she managed to restore some kind of calm. Louis, though, could not be consoled. He was utterly crushed. Writing to her sister-in-law to tell her the fatal news, she begged her not to worry or to be too upset. All was in the hands of God. With a typical touch, she added that she had a corn on one of her toes which hurt her far more than did her breast.

Naturally, though, her brother and his wife bombarded her with letters and, after a few months, she had to plead with them to try not to mention her illness. It was becoming a bore. Let them all ignore it and write about more cheerful subjects. Her own attitude was simple and straightforward: "If God cures me, I shall be very happy, for I really would like to live. It distresses me to have to leave my husband and my children. But I tell myself: 'If I am not cured, it is because it will be better for them that I should leave them.' I so much wish that all this talk about the business would stop. It does no good. We have done all that we can, so let us leave it now in the hands of Providence. If I am not cured it is because God is determined to take me."

Mrs. Martin disliked travel, but she made a pilgrimage to Lourdes. Left to herself, she would have stayed contentedly at home in Alençon and spent her last days in work and prayer, but her family and the priests in her parish insisted that she should seek deliverance at Lourdes. It was less than twenty years since Our Lady had appeared to Bernadette, but the little town in the foothills of the Pyrenees was already a magnet for a steadily growing stream of pilgrims. Mrs. Martin refused to let her husband accompany her. She felt that he—who loved journeys—would try to persuade her to visit other places in an effort to give her pleasure, but death was only a few weeks ahead of her. Time and bodily strength were quickly running out. There could be no thought of sight-seeing. Three of her children went with her: Marie, Pauline and Léonie. By every human standard, the episode was a fiasco—and a most uncomfortable one.

Determined to go on an organized pilgrimage, Mrs. Martin found that one was leaving Angers at just before eight o'clock in the morning of June 18, and she managed to secure the last four tickets for it. With Léonie, she left Aïençon the day before, broke her journey at Le Mans, there collected Marie and Pauline and arrived at Angers in the afternoon. They left for Lourdes next morning. The journey was a nightmare of discomfort. The jolting of the carriage tortured the cancer-wracked body of Mrs. Martin. Other pilgrims in the compartment made themselves coffee on a spirit-stove and upset it all over the food the Martins were carrying with them and on their clothes. A piece of grit flew into Marie's eye and the pain kept her in tears for several hours; Léonie was weeping too because her shoes were too tight. They arrived in Lourdes at five o'clock in the morning.

During the twenty-one hour journey Mrs. Martin got only two hours sleep. There was confusion over the rooms they thought they had booked, and they ended by staying at a convent where the sisters were kind but the food scanty. Marie lost the rosary of Mrs. Martin's dead sister —a deeply upsetting loss for Zélie—and Pauline lost her own rosary. Mrs. Martin slipped down a couple of steps and wrenched her neck badly. The whole pilgrimage was a chapter of misfortunes, none of them serious, yet all painful and harassing to a dying woman. And she was not healed. She plunged four times into the icy water but, as she said: "The Blessed Virgin declared as she did to Bernadette: 'I shall make you happy, not in this world, but in the next.' "

Just after midnight on August 28, 1877, Mrs. Martin died. Marie was seventeen years old, Pauline sixteen,

Léonie fourteen, Céline eight and Thérèse four. Their father was fifty-four. The loss of his wife was a most heavy
blow and it seemed hard that she could not have been
spared until the two youngest children had put on a few
more years. Yet we know that all that happens is willed
by God and so, though rebellion against such an apparent
tragedy is very natural, it is as wrong as it is foolish. It is,
however, not always quickly evident to the intelligence
that catastrophe has within it the seeds of ultimate joy.
Reason often rebels, though faith accepts. Our lives are
short and, within their compass, it may well be that we
cannot see the full design, the completed pattern.

But the death of Mrs. Martin happened nearly a century ago and it is, perhaps, not presumptuous to feel that
at last we can see its purpose and rejoice in it. Volumes
have been written about St. Thérèse, but so far it has not
been sufficiently stressed how all things worked to the end
of making her a saint—and a universally known saint.
Even the defects of the Carmel she entered (and at first,
they were very great) were made to serve this purpose.
Let us consider what followed from Mrs. Martin's death.

Before, the family was happily established in Alençon.
The parents' business was flourishing. The two elder girls
were being educated by Visitation nuns. Léonie was being
taught by nuns in Alençon. So was Céline. And Thérèse
had lessons at home. There was no reason why their lives
should not have continued gently and uneventfully for
several years. What the girls would have done we do not
know. They could have married, entered a convent, or
stayed at home and played a part in the lace business. As
we shall see, Marie had no early inclination towards the
convent, and several young men showed great interest in
Céline.

But whatever had happened, it is certain that, had the
Martins stayed in Alençon, four of the sisters would not
have entered the Carmel in Lisieux. And if they had not,
should we ever have heard of Thérèse? But with the
death of his wife, Mr. Martin thought seriously as to
whether he would be doing the right thing for his children

by keeping them in Alençon, when in Lisieux, Zélie's brother and his wife, with two daughters of their own, were pressing him to settle there and declaring how over-joyed they would be to help supervise the upbringing of their four nieces.

Had he been childless, there is little doubt but that he would have stayed in Alençon, for he was a self-sufficient man and not dependent on human companionship. But his devotion to his children was absolute. Their best inter-ests always overrode his own inclinations. As Marie wrote to her aunt at that time: "He would make any sacrifice for us—his happiness or his life if it were necessary." And so, by the end of November, they were all installed in Les Buissonnets, a house in Lisieux found for them by Mr. Guérin, for Mr. Martin had decided that the well-being of his daughters would be better served there than in Alençon. It was a momentous decision.

Chapter 4

A NEW LIFE—LISIEUX—LOUIS

On the day of Mrs. Martin's funeral, the five children and Louise, the maid, stood in a melancholy group at home. Louise said: "You poor little things; you are without a mother now." Céline flung herself into Marie's arms, exclaiming: "All right, you'll be my mother." Thérèse hurled herself upon Pauline with the words: "And Pauline's going to be my mother." In fact, Marie (who was also Thérèse's godmother) and Pauline joined forces to bring up their two young sisters, but Pauline entered Carmel when Thérèse was getting on toward ten. Marie stayed home until Thérèse was nearly fourteen, so it was Marie who had the most immediate influence over her for the longer time during her schoolgirl days.

It was to Marie that Thérèse could end a letter: "Your very own little daughter who loves you as much as it is possible to love." And it was Marie who was given the task of initiating Thérèse into the ways of Carmel when Thérèse herself entered the convent at Lisieux. We cannot assess the precise amount of influence exercised by each of these sisters but, dearly though Thérèse loved Marie, it was towards Pauline that she turned when inside Carmel, no doubt because Pauline was the more forceful character and because she held the office of prioress during three years of Thérèse's conventual life. Marie and Pauline were, in all but the literal sense, true mothers to Thérèse but, after Mrs. Martin's death, the dominating influence in her life was that exercised by her father.

So far, not a great deal has been heard of him. This is partly because Mrs. Martin naturally played a greater part

in Thérèse's life when she was a little child and partly
too because Mr. Martin disliked writing letters, and this
has deprived us of the wealth of documentation about his
activities, his thoughts, and his feelings that his wife has
provided about herself in the mass of letters which she
wrote. It is also fair to assume that Zélie was the dominating partner of the marriage. Louis was loved and re-
vered as the head of the household, but one has the
feeling that he was overshadowed by the personality of his
wife. Once again, this may be because she is brought so
vividly to life in her letters, and the light she throws keeps
him in the shadows. Certainly he does not emerge clearly
until he establishes himself in Lisieux.

For this period of his life we are fortunate to have his
daughters' memories of him. When she was in her
sixteenth year and had been in Carmel for nearly four
months, Thérèse wrote to him: "The longer I live, my
dearest Father, the more I love you . . . when I think of
you, I naturally think of God, for I cannot believe it
possible to find anyone holier than you in the world. You
are certainly as saintly as St. Louis himself, and I must
keep telling you how much I love you—as if you didn't
know it by now. Oh! How proud I am to be your Queen.
I hope I shall always be worthy of the title . . . I shall always remain your little Queen and I shall try to glorify
you by becoming a great saint." This is not a letter to a
nonentity. No weak, ineffectual figure could win such a
tribute—and it is only one of many—from one who did
indeed become a great saint.

Thérèse lived at Les Buissonnets from November,
1877, until April, 1888, that is, from the age of nearly
five until she just turned fifteen. Les Buissonnets stood on
a steep little path leading off the road from Lisieux to
Trouville. The house could not be seen from the path. Its
garden was entered by a door in a high wall. The house
itself was of red brick with white-painted woodwork. A
large lawn and flower beds stretched in front of it. Behind
was another lawn, a vegetable garden, clumps of laurel

and spindle bushes, a greenhouse, a washhouse, and a large gate to allow the easy delivery of casks of cider and loads of wood and coal.

On the ground floor was the oak-panelled dining room, the kitchen, a small room and a box room; four bedrooms and two dressing rooms comprised the first floor; above them were three attic rooms and the belvedere, a spacious room at the front of the house from whose windows one could see across the town and far into the green, thickly wooded countryside beyond. This was Mr. Martin's place of retreat, a substitute for the Pavilion at Alençon. Thérèse always delighted in Les Buissonnets:

"Everything proved a fresh source of delight. The trim lawn in front of the house, the kitchen garden at the back, the distant view from the large attic windows—all this appealed to my youthful imagination. Its position gave it an added charm, for it stood in a quiet part of the town, within easy reach of a beautiful park laid out with flowers. This charming dwelling was the scene of many family joys which I can never forget."

Let us look at the life she led there. It was austere, and only a little of that austerity came from the fact that the house had neither gas, electricity, nor running water—a not unnatural state of affairs, considering the place and time. It was not the lack of modern conveniences which determined the way of life at Les Buissonnets. The sobriety of existence there was due to the will of Mr. Martin, a will wholeheartedly accepted by his daughters. No fire was ever lit in the bedrooms. There was no drawing room. Food was adequate but plain. There were no gourmets among the Martins. The breakfast cup of chocolate allowed the two younger girls was replaced by onion soup when they grew older. Coffee appeared at lunch only on feast days. When they went to school they found that the other girls, during the mid-morning break, drank a little wine and nibbled at biscuits they had brought from home. Céline and Thérèse ate a piece of dry bread.

Apart from the Guérins, they had scarcely any visitors. Very occasionally Mr. Martin would have one or two priests to dinner. But every Monday morning a crowd of wretchedly poor people would arrive at the door and be given money or food—sometimes both. This—a fixed weekly event—did not prevent other unhappy beggars from appearing on other days of the week. They were never turned away empty-handed. Nor did Mr. Martin ever take a walk without a pocketful of coins, so that he could quietly slip one or two into the hand of any needy person he met. Céline had been for a country walk with her father, and on the way home he stopped at a house and handed some money to a woman sitting by the fire with her children. Céline had never before noticed the house and, when they had left, she asked who the woman was. "She's most unfortunate. From time to time her husband deserts her, leaving her without a penny. So then I come along and help her."

These were his private and casual charities, but he was also a zealous member of the Conference of St. Vincent de Paul and had his regular protégés who never asked his help in vain. His rule was expressed in a line he once wrote to Marie: "Give, always give something, and make people happy." He had, of course, ample means and could easily afford his alms, but a little experience of the world soon teaches one that, in nine cases out of ten, the more a man has the less he gives. Mr. Martin also practiced a form of charity even rarer than that which involves distributing cash. It involves complete indifference to worldly opinion. It is the charity of the Samaritan.

For example: Mr. Martin came across a workman who, stumbling along in a drunken daze, had fallen into a shallow stream. He got him onto his feet, picked up his box of tools, took him by the arm and escorted him home. He was, too, always particularly careful not to offend another person's proper dignity. He went to the dentist to have a tooth out. The dentist did his best, but could make not the slightest impression on the tooth. Ashamed of his failure, he stammered out apologies. Mr. Martin told him not to worry: "I shall not mention a word of this to a soul." Nor did he, except to his daughters.

We are reminded of an incident in the Lisieux Carmel. As a young novice Thérèse delighted in arranging flowers around the statue of the Child Jesus, but they had to be flowers without scent, for the smell of flowers upset one of the old nuns. One day, she was busy arranging a fresh group of flowers and had just placed a rose at the foot of the statue when she heard her name called by this particular nun who had been watching her from a distance. Thérèse knew she was going to object to the rose. "I longed to point out to her that the rose was an artificial one," Thérèse declares, "but Jesus forbade me to enjoy this little triumph. Before she could speak, I picked up the rose, took it to her and said: 'Look, Mother, how marvellously they imitate nature these days. Wouldn't you think I'd just picked this in the garden?'"

Thérèse never had any money of her own, but she realized what would have happened to it if she had: "I should certainly have been ruined, for I couldn't have borne to see anyone destitute without instantly giving him everything he needed." Charity, with the example of it presented by their father, became a swift, instinctive response in all the girls whenever they met distress. Léonie paid constant visits to a woman who was dying alone in a vermin-infested hovel and looked after her tenderly, cleaning the place, washing her, providing her with fresh linen and, when the end came, preparing her body for burial.

If Thérèse had not been cannonized, we should know nothing of the love for the poor and unfortunate that was always alive and active at Les Buissonnets for, while it was operating, few but those who were warmed by it knew of it. But the Church, before raising Thérèse to the altar, rightly insisted on searching out all that could be told of her, and, as she did not exist in a vacuum, the searchlight played across her family. This must be kept in mind lest it should be thought that the inhabitants of Les Buissonnets spent every waking moment jotting down anecdotes with the purpose of showing how fully they practiced the Christian virtues. Their charity was unostentatious but never failing. When he died, the friends of Mr. Martin could say: "His charity was most admirable; he never uttered an unkind judgment about anyone, and he was always ready to excuse the wrongdoing of a neighbor." These were not formal words. They were a simple statement of the truth.

It was in this school of charity that Thérèse had her first lessons. In the summer of 1887, an Italian criminal named Pranzini murdered a woman in Paris, together with her child and maid. He stole the woman's jewels and was caught when trying to sell them. Condemned to death, he spent the time before his execution boasting of his crimes and mocking religion. His crimes were many. The triple murder was the culmination of a life of theft and violence and sexual excess. The newspapers were full of accounts of his exploits.

Somehow, although she was not allowed to read a newspaper, Thérèse heard enough of Pranzini to know that a very great sinner was going to die unrepentant. She exclaimed: "He must be saved from Hell!" So she began to pray for his conversion. Céline, too, joined in this campaign of rescue. Thérèse felt confident that God would answer her prayers, but she begged Him to give her a sign that He had. Pranzini remained defiant and blasphemous almost to the last but, as he was lying strapped on the plank of the guillotine, a second or two before the blade fell, he asked the attendant priest for a crucifix and kissed it three times. Thérèse had been given her sign.

The Martins were never shocked by sinners, never disgusted by them. They were sorry for them and wanted only to help them. Neither Céline nor Thérèse felt any distaste for Pranzini: to them he was a suffering human being in the gravest peril and their only concern was to save him. We see the same attitude still there when Thérèse was a young woman of twenty. Céline and Léonie were living with and looking after Mr. Martin, who was then helpless and deranged in mind. Céline was worried about one of the servants she had discovered to be a thief. Thérèse wrote to her: "Your poor servant is very unfortunate to have such an unpleasant fault, but there is mercy for every sin, and God is powerful enough to give strength to even the weakest person. I'm going to say many prayers for her. In her place, perhaps I should be worse than she is, and she might already be a great saint if she had received half the graces God has showered on me." It never occurred to either Céline or Thérèse to dismiss the woman.

Thérèse's charity came to its full flower in Carmel. There was nothing spectacular about it; in her circumstances there could not be.

There was an old, lame nun, Sister St. Pierre, crotchety and full of grumbles. At evening prayers, Thérèse always knelt behind her, and every evening at ten minutes to six, the old nun had to be helped out of chapel and led to the refectory. No one performed this task to her satisfaction and she grumbled at everyone. Thérèse volunteered for the job. So, for several years, she kept a lookout for the wave of Sister St. Pierre's hourglass, her signal that she was ready to go. Thérèse rose, helped her to her feet and walked behind her, holding her firmly by her girdle to prevent her falling. Having got her safely into the refectory, Thérèse lowered her gently onto the bench, turned back the sleeves of her tunic and, as her hands were twisted with arthritis, cut up her bread for her.

Another nun had a personality which Thérèse found almost unbearable; so, says Thérèse: "I made up my mind to treat her as if I loved her more than anyone in the world." Steadily and deliberately, she settled down to doing this with such success that the unsuspecting nun once asked her at recreation: "Won't you please tell me, Sister Thérèse, what it is about me that attracts you so much?" No one suspected the real position. Even Marie, her sister, was so deceived that she became jealous and complained to Pauline: "I did, when all is said and done, bring her up, yet now she seems to prefer this sister whom I find so unpleasant." And the nun herself could say after Thérèse's death: "Well, at least, I made her really happy when she was alive."

The nun who was the portress irritated almost beyond endurance every assistant she had. She was elderly and never ceased faultfinding. When Thérèse helped her, she, too, felt from time to time that she would not be able to tolerate it a moment longer. But she maintained unbroken a facade of smiling, kindly helpfulness. When another novice succeeded her and protested to the old nun about her manner, she was told: "I don't understand what you are grumbling about. Sister Thérèse never spoke to me like that."

As mentioned earlier, there is nothing dramatic or spectacular about any of this. She never had the opportunity to make some easy, though breathtaking gesture. What she did was far more difficult. Year after year she lived in Carmel and never once lost her temper, never once showed impatience, never once failed to be kind and sympathetic to every other Sister. She said: "When Jesus gave His own commandment to His apostles, He did not tell them to love their neighbor as themselves, but to love them as He loves them, and as He will love them to the End of Time." And that, throughout her life in Carmel, was what she set herself to do.

Mr. Martin never interfered in the day-to-day management of the household. Marie was in charge. She knew what her father's wishes were and she worked within their framework. There was no idleness: each weekday began with attendance at the six o'clock Mass in the Cathedral; Léonie was a boarder at a school in the town run by Benedictine nuns and Céline went there from eight o'clock in the morning until half-past five in the evening; Marie, with the help of a servant, attended to the house and the meals. Pauline did her share, but until Thérèse went to school four years after their arrival in Lisieux, much of her time was taken up in teaching her little sister.

There was always sewing to be done and, apart from the mending of household linen, much fine embroidery was accomplished. Pauline spent two years of her leisure time making a magnificent lace alb for her spiritual director. She also painted minatures on parchment and ivory. Mr. Martin cultivated his garden, made cider, chopped wood, and looked after the hens and rabbits. When he was not working, he prayed and meditated. His activities as a member of the Conference of St. Vincent de Paul gave him added occupation, and he was the moving spirit behind the establishment in Lisieux of the Nocturnal Adoration, a devotion very dear to him during his years in Alençon. And, though he had retired from business, he still had to keep a watchful eye on his investments, though he never gave more time to them than was absolutely necessary. He confessed to Céline that it would be very easy for him to take too great an interest in increasing his capital, but it was a dangerous path to enter on and, as he said, he refused to get involved in the pursuit of such perishable stuff as money.

There were breaks in this routine. Mrs. Guérin, during the summer, often rented for a month or two a villa in Trouville or Deauville, and the Martin girls in turns stayed with her and their two cousins. Occasionally, they visited Alençon for a few days. In fine weather, there were long walks in the countryside and, at times, a carriage was hired for an excursion further afield. Mr. Martin enjoyed these trips, but he always preferred to mingle devotion with the natural pleasures of travel.

One Holy Week was spent with Marie and Léonie in Paris visiting the city's best known churches and shrines. He was fond of travel: he took Céline and Thérèse to Rome and, later, he and a priest went on a long journey through central Europe to Constantinople. This would have been only one of several expeditions had he not been uneasy at being away from his children for too long. When he arrived in Paris on his way to Constantinople, he sent a short letter addressed to all his children. It began: "How good you are to let me set off on this little jaunt. I shall always be grateful to you for it."

His main recreation was fishing, a sport of which he

never tired. Pauline painted his most memorable catches and decorated the walls of the belvedere with them. Much of what he caught was given to Carmel. Thérèse wrote to him after one such gift: "If you only knew what delight your carp, a real monster, gave us. Dinner was held back for a half-hour and Marie made a delicious sauce for it." When she was a little girl, he often took Thérèse with him to the river: "Sometimes I tried to fish with my own little rod, but I preferred to sit amidst the grass and flowers. I thought deeply then and, although I was quite ignorant about meditation, my soul did plunge into a state of real prayer . . . the rustling of the breeze and half-heard music from a military band filled me with a gentle melancholy. Earth seemed to me a place of exile and I dreamt of heaven."

Thérèse's years at Les Buissonnets have a golden glow about them—particularly those years before she went to school when she was eight and a half. Her mornings were spent working at her lessons under the supervision of Pauline. Catechism and biblical history were her favorite subjects. She was never very good at arithmetic, and grammar caused her much trouble. One of her little essays has survived: "The Blessed Virgin went to the Temple when she was three years old. She stood out amidst her companions by her piety and her angelic sweetness. Everyone loved and admired her, the angels most of all for they thought of her as their little sister. I want to be a very good little girl. The Blessed Virgin is my beloved mother and little children usually take after their mother."

Lessons finished, she ran up to her father in the belvedere to report on her progress. If she had not worked hard or well enough, Pauline made her stay in and do more work in the afternoon—a severe punishment both for her and her father, for it was the delight of both of them to go out together every afternoon, sometimes, as we have seen, upon a fishing expedition, or for a walk in the country or perhaps for a stroll around a little park not far from the house. The afternoon always ended with a visit to the Blessed Sacrament, the elderly white-haired man and Thérèse going hand-in-hand to each of the town's churches in turn.

When she had been particularly industrious at her lessons, Pauline would give her an extra mark, and when enough of these had accumulated, she had a whole day's holiday. When those days fell in the summer when the late afternoons and early evenings were bright and sunny, Thérèse would have her walk in the morning and spend the rest of the day playing in the garden. She had many pets: a spaniel named Tom, rabbits, goldfish, a magpie which ended a life of extreme naughtiness by flying into a waterbutt and drowning itself, and silkworms, many of which met an untimely death when, during Thérèse's absence on holiday in Trouville, Céline had given them the wrong kind of leaves to eat.

She was not very fond of dolls, but enjoyed seeing Céline playing with hers and loved it when Céline took them over to her, urging them to hug their aunt. Among her toys were a wooden top, a trumpet, a skipping-rope, a see-saw, a small wheelbarrow, a model sailing-boat, a kaleidoscope, and miniature tea and dinner services. From one of her tiny cups her father had often to pretend to drink a curious brew she made from seeds and leaves and bits of bark, and he was frequently taken to a little patch of garden she tended to admire its flowers and the toy altars she built in a recess in the wall which ran along one end of it.

The name of Thérèse rang round the garden so often that a parrot in a house beyond the wall was soon croaking; "Thérèse! Thérèse!" and giving the "r's" the authentic French trill. One day Mr. Martin, having come into a little money unexpectedly, decided to give a hundred francs to each of his daughters, so he hid the packets of gold pieces in various spots in the garden and set them hunting for them with cries of: "Now you're getting warm . . . no, you're going to freeze."

But perhaps winter evenings were the best times of all.

Dinner was eaten, the table cleared and the washing-up done. Thérèse ran to the bottom of the stairs and shouted: "Papa! Papa! The lamp is lit." Mr. Martin came downstairs and they all settled down in a room adjoining the kitchen. The lamp shone warmly and the logs crackled in the grate. Marie played a game of checkers with her father, then either he or one of the girls would read passages from *The Liturgical Year* and there would be a general discussion about them; perhaps Mr. Martin would produce from one of his pockets another of the many little toys he made—great favorites were figures whittled from elder pith and weighted at the bottom with a pellet of lead so that they always bounced up again whenever they were knocked down. Thérèse was fascinated by them and Mr. Martin told her: "In all the troubles of life, you must behave like these good little fellows and spring up after every tumble."

Céline and Thérèse often climbed onto his knee, and he sang them songs of his youth. Sometimes he picked up Thérèse and seated her in solitary state on his knee and delighted her by quoting a line from a dialect poem: "My goodness, here is my little Queen who has made the fortune of everyone in the Auvergne," mouthing every syllable very slowly and distinctly. He had pet names for all his children. Thérèse was "the little Queen of France and Navarre," the "orphan of Berezina," the "little blonde may-bug;" Marie was his "diamond," his "first," "the gypsy;" Pauline his "fine pearl;" Léonie "the good," and Céline "the fearless." On these lamplit winter evenings, after the reading and the games, there might be a feast of chestnuts roasted in front of the fire. Bedtime finally came and the day ended as it had begun, with prayers.

No shadow of unhappiness touched Thérèse during these early years spent, as they were, in childish work and play, conducted in an atmosphere of sympathy and love. It is easy to imagine she was badly spoiled. That she was not is entirely due to Pauline and Marie. She herself said that no fault was ever passed over, and once a decision had been made, it was never changed. She was expected to give complete and instant obedience to any order. She never found it hard to obey: "Even when I was a very young child, it was never necessary to scold me. One gentle word was enough to make me understand that I had done wrong and to be sorry for it. It has been the same all my life."

Neither Céline nor Thérèse—when she went to school—was ever allowed to stay away from her lessons because of minor illnesses, and all complaints about trivial aches and pains were sharply discouraged. So it is not surprising that when she was a Carmelite she was often in the choir chanting the Divine Office although suffering acute pain and nausea from stomach trouble. When Céline remonstrated with her, her reply—given with a smile—was: "Well, if I do collapse, they'll be sure to find me."

It was well understood in Les Buissonnets that, if any dispute arose between the servants and the children, it was the children who were wrong and must apologize. A great friend of Thérèse was Victoire, one of these servants. One day Thérèse wanted an inkwell which stood on the kitchen mantlepiece: "As I was too small to reach it, I very politely asked Victoire to give it to me. She refused, telling me to stand on a chair and get it myself. I didn't say a word, but got a chair. I thought, though, that she was behaving unkindly, and I wanted her to know that I thought so. When she was cross with me she used to call me a 'little brat,' a term which annoyed and humiliated me very much. So before jumping down from the chair, I turned to her in a dignified manner and said: 'Victoire, you're a brat!' Then I ran off, leaving her to ponder over my profound remark. I hadn't long to wait for the result, for I soon heard her shouting: 'Mademoiselle Marie, Thérèse has just called me a brat.' Marie appeared and at once made me apologize—but I didn't feel a bit sorry."

Sundays were great days for Thérèse although, as we have seen, melancholy crept over her as they drew to an end. She was allowed to get up later than on weekdays and was given the great treat of having her cup of chocolate in bed, brought up to her by Pauline. Marie did her hair and there were sometimes tears when her curls were pulled too tight. The whole family went off to High Mass. Thérèse sat next to her father and listened attentively to the sermon even though she did not understand much of it. There were walks in the afternoon and then compline.

One or two of the girls spent the evening with their uncle and aunt. Thérèse was pleased when it was her turn. She could sit for hours listening to her uncle talking, but she was terrified with, one imagines, that delicious terror young children so often enjoy, when he took her on his knee and, rolling his eyes ferociously, sang a ballad called "Bluebeard" in a deep, rumbling voice. Mr. Martin came to escort her home, and walking through the quiet, ill-lit streets of the town, she would gaze at the sky, catch sight of the T-shaped constellation of Orion's Belt, and excitedly point it out to her father, telling him: "There's my name written in the sky."

The seclusion of life at Les Buissonnets, the almost complete withdrawal of its occupants from the world are not something we can or should try to imitate. Practically all of us must be involved with the world; we have jobs to do, businesses to run, professions to follow, and we cannot withdraw from the daily hurly-burly. We should be failing in our duty to God and to our neighbor if we tried to. From St. Paul until now, there have been great saints whose lives were spent in the thick of human bustle. They knew all its blood and tears and sweat. God, however, chose a different vocation for St. Thérèse. He put straight lines upon her experience on earth so that she suffered no distractions in preparing herself for endless activity exercised from Heaven. He kept her empty so that He could fill her with love for Himself. She said: "God has mercifully allowed me to know only just enough of the world to make me despise it and flee from it."

She was hidden and insignificant in this world, but as

she said: "A very tiny spark can set a huge light ablaze in the Church, just as its doctors and martyrs have done." As she drew nearer death, she knew that her work was about to begin. With a splendid certainty she declared: "I shall pass my time in heaven doing good upon earth ... I shall not be able to have any rest until the End of the World and so long as there are souls to save."

Chapter 5

RELIGIOUS FORMATION

Bombing, as the last war drew to an end, destroyed the greater part of Lisieux. Until then it had been one of the showplaces of Normandy, much of it a network of narrow, torturous streets lined with medieval houses superbly adorned with wooden carvings, illustrating the piety and fantasy of long dead craftsmen. "Warm, living relics of the Middle Ages" was one description given to these streets.

Nowhere is it recorded that Mr. Martin and his daughters noticed them. For the Martins lacked any aesthetic sense. Painting, sculpture, architecture, music, literature—all meant nothing to them. Mr. Martin's books, apart from the Scriptures and the *Imitation of Christ,* were lives of the saints and books of piety, and he knew by heart a few of the more sentimental poems of Chateaubriand, Hugo and Lemartine. He refused to read any novels. By the end of her life, Thérèse was steeped in the Scriptures, the *Imitation,* the writings of St. John of the Cross and St. Teresa. She knew little else. When she and Céline were together in Carmel, they looked at one of the bookshelves and Thérèse burst out: "How sorry I should be if I'd read all those books. What a headache they'd have given me and how much valuable time I'd wasted that I've spent in loving God." Towards the end of her life she said: "The Gospels alone are enough for me. I no longer find anything worthwhile in other books."

Before she entered Carmel she read a few books, but most of them were of no great merit. Yet we find that the legend is still maintained that her reading was wide and deep. She enjoyed Wiseman's *Fabiola* in translation, and

59

there were books such as *Ernestine or the Charms of Nature, The Young Workers or Trial and Recompense, The History of Chivalry, The Holiday of a Christian Girl or A Practical Guide to a Well-Spent Holiday.* In Carmel she read a handful of saints' lives, an essay by Bossuet, two books by the English Oratorian, Father Frederick Faber, and a few other volumes of spirituality.

She had not a great deal of free time: by the Rule there were two periods each day—one of a half-hour and one of an hour—which the professed nuns could devote to spiritual reading. But the novices had to spend the half-hour with the novice-mistress and so Thérèse, either as a novice or acting novice-mistress, was always occupied throughout this period. As for the hour, much of it was spent by her in letter writing or in composing her verses, which were often written to satisfy the demand of one or other of the nuns. Yet, had she had the time, she would not have read much: "Sometimes, my poor little brain gets tired very quickly when I read some of the spiritual treatises which shows perfection surrounded by a thousand obstacles. So I close the learned book which makes my head ache and withers my heart, and I pick up the Bible. Then everything becomes clear, and a single word reveals infinite horizons and perfection seems easy." The older she grew the more completely satisfied she was with Holy Scripture. She wanted nothing more.

As we have just seen, the range of her reading was very limited, but four books had a most profound influence upon her. *The Imitation of Christ,* by Thomas à Kempis is the first of them. Before she was fourteen, she knew it by heart and her aunt, Mrs. Guérin, often opened the book, read the first words of a chapter and Thérèse would take them up and recite the whole chapter without hesitation. On the very day she entered Carmel, the prioress spoke to her about the book and, at her demand, Thérèse declaimed without a mistake the famous chapter on the love of Christ. In *The Story of a Soul* she quotes from *The Imitation* forty times. In it she read: "Love to be unknown and esteemed as nothing ... let me be possessed by love, rising above myself through excess of fervor and ecstasy," and she learned of the vanity of this world and of the splendor that awaits the servants of God. She read there of the need to receive Holy Communion frequently: "How happy is he and acceptable to God who so liveth and keepeth his conscience in such purity as to be ready and well disposed to communicate every day," and she had not forgotten those words when she wrote: "Jesus does not come down from Heaven every day in order to stay in a golden ciborium, but to find another Heaven in our souls." She insisted that Holy Communion was not the reward of virtue but essential food for contrite sinners.

This, joined with her love of Holy Scripture, reminds one of Thomas à Kempis: "For in this life I find there are two things especially necessary for me, without which this miserable life would be insupportable. Whilst I am kept in the prison of the body I acknowledge that I need two things—food and light. Thou hast, therefore, given to me, weak as I am, Thy sacred Body for the nourishment of my soul and body, and Thou hast set 'Thy word as a lamp to my feet.' " And how fully, in her life, were these words of his proved: "Never read anything that thou mayest appear more learned or more wise. When thou shalt have read and learnt many things, thou must always return to recognize that I am He who teacheth men knowledge and that I give a more clear understanding to little ones than can be taught by man. He to whom I speak will quickly be wise and will make great progress in spiritual matters."

A second book had an effect upon her impossible to overestimate: *The End of this World and the Mysteries of the Future Life.* It contained nine sermons delivered by the Abbé Arminjon, a former professor of Scripture and ecclesiastical history at the college of Chambéry. The sermons were delivered in the Cathedral of the town, and they were published in 1881. Thérèse says: "The book was lent to my father by the Carmel. I did not usually read his books, but I asked if I could borrow this one. It was one of the great graces of my life. I read it sitting by the window of my room, and I cannot describe the impression it made on me, so sweet and intimate was it. I copied out several passages on the perfection of love and on how God would receive His chosen at the moment when He became their great and eternal reward. I read over and over again about His love, and my heart was set ablaze. I was carried away by the great truths of religion and the mysteries of eternity." And again: "The reading of this book filled me with heavenly delight and I felt a foretaste of what God has in store for those who love Him. When I realized how great was the gap between the rewards of eternity and the trifling sacrifices we make in this life, I determined to love Jesus with every ounce of my being and to give Him endless tokens of my life whilst I still could."

One of the passages she copied out was: "Ah! God cannot forget that His saints, during their life on earth, paid Him homage by sacrificing their rest, their earthly pleasures and their whole being, that they longed to be able to pour out their blood in an inexhaustible stream as a living witness of their faith; that they desired to have each a thousand hearts so that they could all be consumed with the ardor of their love, and that they longed for a thousand bodies to be martyred. And God will cry: 'Now it is My turn! As the saints gave Me themselves, can I do anything less than give them Myself in My entirety? It is a great deal to make them lords of creation and to envelop them in the blaze of My splendor, but it is certainly not the most My Heart will do. I owe them more than Paradise, more than the treasures of My Wisdom; I owe them My eternal and infinite Being. If I take into My house My servants and My friends, if I comfort them and embrace them with My charity, their desires will be overwhelmingly satisfied and they will have received more than enough to give them perfect peace of heart, but it is not enough to content My Heart or to give perfect satisfaction to My Love. I must be the soul of their soul by penetrating them through and through with My Divinity, even as iron is made white-hot by fire. I must show myself to them without a cloud or veil, without the intervention of the senses; I must unite Myself to them face to face and let My Glory so irradiate them that it shines from all their being so that they know Me as I know them and they themselves become as gods.' " With what delight Thérèse must have pondered over passages such as this, absorbing them and making them her own.

We cannot read Abbé Arminjon's volume of sermons: it went into two editions and now has disappeared. A copy may possibly be lying, forgotten and unread, stained and dusty, on some dark shelf of a monastic library; one may turn up in the book-boxes along the Seine; or every volume may have travelled to the dust-bin or furnace along the path worn smooth by so many collections of printed sermons. It would be a splendid discovery if a copy were found, but it is not a matter of real importance. The book has done its work and the Abbé, an instrument in the hand of God, now knows the true worth of the sermons he preached so long ago.

Thérèse says that, between the age of seventeen and eighteen, she read nothing but the works of St. John of the Cross. She had, too, a particular devotion to her patron saint, St. Teresa of Avila. She read some of her writings and, of course, knew intimately the Rule and the Constitutions of Carmel which St. Teresa drew up and about which she said to her nuns on the day before she died: "For the love of God I ask you to observe the Rule and the Constitutions well; if you keep them strictly, no further miracle will be necessary for your canonization." St. Teresa, the Foundress of the Reformed Carmel, and St. John of the Cross, her friend and the Order's Spiritual Doctor, have in St. Thérèse their most faithful and their greatest daughter.

Some of the writers about St. Thérèse would have us believe that the saint herself and her sisters had great artistic talent. Certainly Pauline, Céline and Thérèse drew and painted, as did thousands of other girls of their time. Such activity was considered a genteel pursuit for young ladies who were not of the working class, but to confuse these outpourings with art is to show a complete absence of sensibility. The productions of the Martin girls are quite without distinction and so are the verses written by St. Thérèse.

On her pilgrimage to Rome Thérèse stopped in Milan. The city's great cemetery is a sad place for any artist, crammed as it is with white marble statues of angels, of children strewing petals on graves, of weeping maidens, broken columns, melancholy doves and the like. Thérèse liked the cemetery better than the Cathedral, and she described the statues as masterpieces.

It is only fair to add that Thérèse had no illusions about herself. From Rome she wrote to one of her cousins: "You know Italy is the country of artists. You could judge what is beautiful better than I can, for I am certainly no artist. There is nothing for me in Rome. Everything is for artists." This indifference to visual art was shared by the whole Martin family. One has only to visit the tomb of St. Thérèse in the Carmel of Lisieux. It is a sculptural abomination, yet Pauline was governing the Carmel as prioress for life when it was designed and manufactured.

Politics might not have existed for all the attention the Martins gave it. A brief mention of the Franco-Prussian War in a letter by Mrs. Martin and an expression of horror at the shooting of hostages by the Paris Commune is all that was ever said by any of them about the events that were reshaping Europe. They would have found it difficult to discover what was going on in the world, for Mr. Martin took only one paper, *La Croix,* a Catholic daily then more concerned with theological polemics and ecclesiastical news than with secular politics, and even that paper, harmless enough one would think, was not allowed to be read by the younger girls.

Ignorant of nearly everything untraveled and without friends—this was the position of the five girls in Lisieux. They lived within the walls of the garden of Les

Buissonnets, emerging only to go to church, to school, to shop and, on Sunday evenings, to visit their aunt and uncle. As we have seen, they made very infrequent excursions into the countryside during the summer months. It would seem to be an existence so limited, so circumscribed as to destroy the happiness of any young people forced to endure it, but it was, instead, the framework within which were laid the foundations of Thérèse's sanctity and within which all of them knew intense happiness.

For their lives were not empty and were not spent in isolation. "God with His holy angels will draw nigh to him who withdraweth himself from his acquaintances and friends" are the words of Thomas à Kempis and, at Lisieux, it was God who filled what would otherwise have been a spiritual and mental vacuum. These girls, so out of touch with the world, were in touch with the ultimate, eternal reality, not with the ephemeral shadows of the world. So how could they be lonely? They loved God; everything they did was meant to please Him; and they were sure that He loved them even as their father did. As Thérèse said:

"If I possessed all the treasures of this world, I should be wretched, for my heart would be so empty. It's incredible how big my heart seems when I think of these treasures, as all of them piled up together could not content it. Yet how tiny it seems when I think of Jesus!"

This was when she was sixteen. Her mother said of her when she was four: "She talks of nothing but God and she never fails to say her prayers." Her dying words were: "Oh! I love Him! My God, I love You!" Her sisters' lives are not so well documented, neither were they so eloquent or so passionate but, as far as they were capable, they thought and felt as Thérèse did. Perhaps they could not say, as she did: "I don't believe I've ever spent more than three minutes at a time without thinking of God, for surely one thinks all the time of someone a person loves dearly."

Few people could, but her sisters' awareness of God's presence was sharp and as constant as is possible for human nature, unless it enjoys the special graces of a Thérèse. So it is absurd to imagine that they were ever bored or discontented within the narrow round of their daily lives. Without God, it would have been insupportable; claustrophobia would have destroyed them; with God, their lives were full and overflowing with joy and they knew the freedom that He alone can give, one that is unimaginable to those fettered by the world's chains.

Chapter 6

LES BUISSONNETS—SCHOOL—
HER SISTERS JOIN RELIGION

"My life at Les Buissonnets went on in peace and happiness and I was enveloped in love." So said Thérèse, writing of herself when she was about eight. "But," she went on, "I was now old enough to begin the struggle of life and to get to know the world and the tragedies with which it is filled." Big and serious words and not really justified by the events she describes, if we put these events alongside the struggles and tragedies that most human beings experience. But we must realize that to any sensitive young girl living completely sheltered from the normal rough and tumble of life, the happenings of the next two or three years must have come as an overwhelming shock. Thérèse was very nearly overwhelmed.

When she was eight and a half, her sister, Léonie, left school and Thérèse became a pupil. Céline was already one. Thérèse and Céline were not boarders as Marie and Pauline had been at Le Mans. They were day girls, leaving home early each morning and returning in the late afternoon. Like so many children, Thérèse had often heard it said that one's schooldays were the best and happiest years one would ever know, but "not for me they weren't. The five years I spent at school were the most wretched of my life. If Céline hadn't been there with me, I could not have stood it for a single month without being ill."

At this stage in her life, Thérèse was quite incapable of getting on with people other than members of her family. The girls at her convent school had been brought up very differently, and though they were all girls of a similar or higher class than Thérèse, they must have seemed tough little hoydens, and she knew neither how to ingratiate herself with them nor how to dominate them. For one thing, she had never learned to play with other children, nor did she like the ordinary, lively games of childhood. She tells how bored she was when a whole afternoon was spent in dancing quadrilles, and she passed many a recreation period leaning against a tree, lost in thought—behavior which would not endear her to any children in any school at any time.

One macabre game she invented herself. Dead birds were found from time to time lying under the trees; she enjoyed burying them. A few other girls began to help her, and they soon had a cemetery planted with cuttings and flowers of a size suitable for the tiny bodies. She had some success, too, in telling stories and was often surrounded by a ring of girls, but a mistress quickly put a stop to that, saying that recreation was meant for playing and running about, not for standing chattering.

Pauline had taught her well, so she was put in a class where every other girl was her senior. That did not increase her popularity. She shone at history, essay-writing and religious knowledge. When she went home in the evening, she usually had some scholastic success to report to her father—such as the one when she would have received full marks for an essay if she had not forgotten the name of Moses' father, though it was the best essay turned in by her class, and she was given a silver brooch for it. Mr. Martin always rewarded these successes with a coin. Pauline gave her a hoop to encourage her to continue working hard. Thérèse says: "I really needed such tokens of love, for without them life at school would have been unendurable."

A greater shock than her introduction to school life was ahead. Since early childhood Pauline had wanted to become a nun, and when Thérèse started school, she felt that she was free to follow this vocation. She thought only of entering the Visitation Convent at Le Mans where she had been educated. She was twenty and resigned herself to staying in the world a little longer when the Visitation prioress told her she could not be admitted until she was twenty-two. However, on February 16, 1882, she, her father and Marie went to six o'clock Mass in the chapel of Our Lady of Carmel in the Church of St. Jacques, and there she suddenly and very strongly felt certain that God wished her to become a Carmelite. She said: "I had *never* before thought of Carmel."

The moment she got home, she took Marie aside and told her what had happened. Marie warned her of the austerity of Carmel, saying she did not think her health was good enough to endure it. Later in the day, Pauline confided in her father. He, too, spoke very much as Marie had done, "But I saw that he was really very proud that I had this vocation." Towards evening, she met him as he was going upstairs. He stopped her: "You mustn't think, dear Pauline, that because I am happy to give you to God I shall not suffer at your leaving me, for I love you dearly."

She discussed the matter with her spiritual director and with her uncle and aunt. No one opposed her desire. But she did not tell Thérèse: "My silence grievously wounded her sensitive heart. If only I had realized how much I made her suffer, I would have told her everything. For, though she was only nine, she had wisdom beyond her years, but I never suspected it. Yet I console myself by thinking that my mistake served the purposes of God. The graces that came afterwards prove that."

Thérèse learned that she was to lose Pauline when she overheard her talking to Marie about Carmel. She did not know what Carmel was, but she did grasp that Pauline was going to leave her and enter a convent, and that she was to be deprived of her "second mother." Thérèse declares: "In a flash, I realized what life was like. Until then it had not seemed too miserable a business, but then I saw what it really was—nothing but suffering and continual partings. I wept bitterly, for then I didn't understand the joy of sacrifice. I was weak, so weak that I thought it a great grace to be able to endure a trial which seemed far beyond my strength. If the news of Pauline's departure had been broken to me gently, I shouldn't have suffered anything like as much, but coming on me as a complete surprise, it was like having a sword plunged into my heart."

With great tenderness Pauline tried to comfort her, explaining to her what Carmel was and the kind of life that went on there. To Thérèse it sounded wonderful: "When I thought it over, I felt that Carmel was the desert in which He wanted me also to hide myself."

Sometime before, she had told Pauline that she wished to spend her life in solitude and had asked her if she would go with her to some far away desert. Pauline, speaking to a child, said she felt the same but that she would wait before setting out until Thérèse was old enough to go with her. Thérèse had taken her seriously, which partly accounts for her distress when she heard of Carmel, but once she saw Carmel as the desert for which she had longed, she felt a "great peace." She says the feeling that she was destined for Carmel was not a childish dream. She was certain she was being called by God and declares: "I wanted to enter Carmel, not because of Pauline, but solely for the sake of Jesus." One wonders.

Thérèse wrote these words when she was twenty-two, and by then she had proved over and over again that her family counted for nothing alongside Our Lord. She loved her sisters dearly, yet she was willing, eager even, to leave them and go to a Carmel in Indo-China if it had been God's will. We know that she was an extraordinary child, but even so, it is difficult, almost impossible, to believe that when she heard that her sister, a sister she loved more than anyone in the world, was entering Carmel, she also decided to enter without that decision being influenced by the knowledge that it would reunite her with Pauline.

But Thérèse undoubtedly believed it thirteen years later. There is no reason why we should feel uneasy if we are driven to think that the prime initial motive impelling her to Carmel was Pauline's entry. Now a canonized saint, refulgent with the light of heaven, she was then, however, still a human being and subject to emotions all creatures feel. Pauline believed that God intervened to send her to Carmel, rather than to the Visitation nuns. That she then became the agent through which He acted to move Thérèse is most fitting, and there is no need for our hesitating to accept the fact that at first it was love for Pauline, rather than the love of God, which made Thérèse so eager to become a Carmelite.

Why should there be? Her love for Pauline was a very natural and a very proper emotion. And it was soon to be swallowed up by her growing, maturing love of God, for in a year or two, she would have been able to say in all truth that her longing for a cell in Carmel was fed by no human yearnings. Her interior life deepened at an amazing pace. But, even with such a spiritually precocious child as Thérèse, we cannot expect a total immolation of self at the age of nine.

She told Pauline that she, too, meant to enter Carmel, and Pauline promised to take her to see the prioress. They went on a Sunday and the prioress, Mother Marie de Gonzague, talked with Thérèse, assured her that she had a vocation, but explained that postulants were never taken at the age of nine. She would have to wait until she was sixteen.

During the few weeks in the world left to Pauline, Céline and Thérèse gave her hardly a moment's peace. Every day they presented her with a cake and some candies, telling themselves that she would soon never be able to eat them again, and they followed her everywhere around the house and garden. At last came the day of her departure to Carmel.

It was October 2, a day which Thérèse calls one of "tears and blessings." In the weeks that followed, Thérèse began to suffer from headaches. No one took much notice of them and she continued to go to school. Next year, Mr. Martin took Marie and Léonie to Paris at Easter, and Céline and Thérèse stayed with their aunt. One evening,

Thérèse was seized with a fit of shivering and was put to bed with plenty of blankets and hotwater bottles. The doctor, called in next day, said she was seriously ill, and she was still in bed when Mr. Martin returned from Paris. Marie stayed with her, for she was not well enough to be taken home. It was getting near the time for Pauline's clothing and no one thought that Thérèse would be able to be present at the ceremony, but she felt quite sure she would be fit to go.

The day of the clothing arrived—April 6—and Thérèse's illness was suspended, so that she was able to have the bitter-sweet joy of seeing Pauline in her wedding dress as a bride of Christ, of sitting on her knee and almost suffocating her with hugs and kisses. After it was all over, a carriage took her home to Les Buissonnets and next day she was as ill as ever. No name was ever given to her complaint, but it was obviously what we, in non-technical terms, would call a nervous breakdown and one which was, equally obviously, caused by the destruction of her secure, familiar world.

She suffered from hallucinations and delirium, and her body was racked and twisted by violent contortions. At times she beat her head against the wooden frame of the bed and once flung herself out of the bed and onto the floor. Her condition grew worse until May 13. (It was on the same date thirty-four years later that Our Lady made her first appearance to the little shepherds of Fatima.) Some days before, Mr. Martin had sent money to Paris for Masses to be said for her in the famous Church of Our Lady of Victories, and the novena was drawing to an end on this Sunday morning. In the sickroom was a statue of Our Lady, nearly three feet high, a copy of a well-known madonna which stood in the Paris church of St. Sulpice until the Revolution. Thérèse has told what happened:

"Marie went into the garden, leaving me with Léonie, who was reading near the window. After a while I began to call very softly for Marie: 'Mama! Mama!' Léonie was used to hearing me call continually for Marie and took no notice, so I began to raise my voice and at last Marie came in. I distinctly saw her enter, but I failed to recognize her and I went on crying more and more loudly: 'Mama! Mama!' I suffered an agony of torment and Marie's suffering was perhaps even sharper. After trying to convince me that she was at my side, she knelt by my bed along with Léonie and Céline and, turning towards the statue of Our Lady, she prayed to her with all the fervor of a mother pleading for the life of her child. And I, having found no help on earth, also turned towards my heavenly Mother and begged her with all my heart to have pity on me. Suddenly the statue took on a beauty beyond anything I had ever seen. The look upon Our Lady's face was indescribably kind and sweet and compassionate, but it was her gracious smile which moved the very depths of my soul. Instantly all my pains vanished, my eyes filled and big tears fell silently, tears of purest heavenly joy." She was cured.

The next big happening in her life was her First Communion. For many months before, Marie and Pauline (from Carmel) had been preparing her. Pauline wrote regularly to her and composed a little book to help her to make a good Communion, and Marie seated her upon her knee and instructed her day after day: "She explained to me that I could become a saint by being faithful over the smallest things." Less than three months before she died, Thérèse was asked by Pauline to explain what she meant by her "little way," which she had declared she would teach to souls after her death.

Her reply was: "It is the way of spiritual childhood, the path of confidence and complete abandon. I want to teach them to make use of the little methods which have succeeded so perfectly with me, to tell them that there is only one thing they have to do down here: to throw to Our Lord the flowers of their little sacrifices."

She made her First Communion on May 8, 1884: "How my soul rejoiced in that first kiss of Jesus. It was a kiss of love. I knew that I was loved and I said to Him: 'I love You and I give myself to You forever' . . . there were no longer two of us. Thérèse had vanished like a drop of water in the ocean. Only Jesus remained, Master and King."

Confirmation followed. In the summer of that year, Céline finished her education, so in the autumn term Thérèse returned to school without her: "I promptly fell ill. The only thing I liked about school was that Céline and I were together. I could not possibly stay there without her." She was taken out and for eleven months visited a Madame Papineau for private lessons. During those months she had only sixty-four lessons, most of them lasting not more than an hour.

Madame Papineau lived with her mother and a cat which usually jumped on the table and sat on Thérèse's books. The room was crammed with furniture, books and papers. Visitors were always popping in, and Thérèse was often distracted—enjoyably as she admits—from her lessons by the gossip going on around her. When these lessons ended, so did her formal education. So, compared with her sisters and most girls of a similar class, she was poorly educated.

In October, 1886, Marie entered Carmel. For many years she had thought of the religious life. It would have been difficult not to in her circumstances, but she had always come to the same decision: it was not the life for her. She was regarded by her family as the strong-willed daughter who had a lively desire to be independent. One of the Martins' servants, Louise, was very strict with the children, sometimes unjustly so, but Marie refused to put up with anything approaching bullying. Every time the maid gave her an unfair order, she said: "Leave me alone, Louise. I am not a slave!" She herself tells this story: "When I was a little girl I hated having to bow to acquaintances we met in the street. I felt humiliated. One day, when we were on our way to the Pavilion, we passed some people we knew and I turned my face away from them, behaving like a little savage. My mother was very upset and told me that if I behaved like that no one would ever love me. But this warning only strengthened my pride. I thought that I would have to bow to be loved and I felt furious at the idea of having to beg for love. I decided I would have none of that and I told my mother: 'As long as you love me, I don't care whether or not other people do.'"

When she left school in her sixteenth year, she was as resolved to hold on to what she called her freedom as she had been in her clashes with Louise. Her aunt, the Visitation nun, urged her to pray daily to St. Joseph and gave her a card with a prayer printed on it. Marie read the prayer but saw that it was described as a special one for priests and nuns. Her instant reaction was: "That's a fine thing! My aunt obviously wants me to be a nun. Well, there's no danger that I shall ever say this prayer!" At the age of twenty-two she was still of the same mind. She tells how she was changed:

"Someone we knew spoke enthusiastically about a Jesuit priest, Father Pichon, who was soon coming to Lisieux to give a retreat—'He's a real saint, a priest such as one rarely meets.' Out of curiosity, I went to see 'the saint.' I heard him say Mass and then went to his confessional, wondering if I should make my confession or tell him the real reason for my visit. I decided to tell the truth and said to him: 'Father, I have come to you so that I can see a saint.' He laughed: 'Very well, my child. Now make your confession.' I did and left without saying any more. As I walked home, I thought I'd really gone out of my way for nothing.

"But that same evening I felt a great longing to see this priest again, and next day I went to his Mass and again entered his confessional: 'Father, I have been driven to come to you again, but I don't know why.' He asked me if I wanted to be a nun. 'No, Father.' 'Do you want to get married?' Oh, no! Certainly not!' 'Well then? But look, I'm in a great hurry, for I have to catch a train. I shall, though, be back in Lisieux in a fortnight and I will have a talk with you then. Meanwhile, write down your impressions of what you think life as a nun is like and say why it doesn't attract you. And put down all you think about what your vocation might be. I strongly hope that I can give you to Jesus.'

"I went back to Les Buissonnets with a light heart and full of a secret joy. On the appointed day I saw Father Pichon, taking with me the eight large pages I had written about my most intimate feelings, and when I had made my confession, I passed them to him through the grill. I was going to get up and go, but he kept me for an hour, reading the manuscript aloud and commenting on it. I felt extremely embarrassed. I had never wanted a spiritual director, but now I had one. And I had chosen him myself, or rather God Himself had chosen him for me. All this was going on at the time Pauline was about to enter Carmel . . . afterwards he wrote to me from time to time, but he was so busy with his usual correspondence and his retreats—he preached more than nine hundred—that there were often long periods when he didn't reply to my letters. I once wrote him fourteen and never had a word from him!"

In 1884, Father Pichon was sent to Canada. He returned to France temporarily in 1886, and it was during this stay that he convinced Marie to delay no longer in seeking admission to Carmel. When she told her father, "God could not have asked me to make a greater sacrifice," he exclaimed, "I thought that you were the one who would never leave me." Her uncle and aunt were astonished, for they knew that in the past she had always said she could not endure life in a convent.

When she walked into Carmel as a postulant on October 15, 1886, she felt no enthusiasm. The courtyard struck her as an exceedingly bare and austere place and the garden a mean, tiny affair compared to the great enclosure of the Visitation convent where she was educated. Everything seemed poverty-stricken—not, one would think, a very remarkable state of affairs in any Carmel. Yet it came as an unpleasant shock to Marie, used to the solid middle-class comfort of Les Buissonnets. She did not even feel any pleasure at being reunited with Pauline. The only thing in her mind was a nagging question: how on earth could she possibly spend the rest of her life within the Carmel walls? Yet, when she was an elderly woman, she could say: "I found Our Lord within these four walls and, in finding Him, I found Heaven. It is here that I have spent the happiest years of my life."

Marie lived to the age of seventy-nine. She never held the positon of prioress, sub-prioress or novice-mistress. Her life was hidden and holy. When she instructed Thérèse before her little sister's First Communion, she taught her a simple and direct devotion, and to the end of her long life she never had any patience with subtle and complicated methods of approaching God.

In a book she read she came across a passage which said that anyone seeking the mystical state of union with God must, at all costs, keep absolute control over his spiritual strength and will. "But," she asked, "what must I do? I have no strength—only weakness. Well, I turn to my little Thérèse. She alone shows me the way. She alone shows me the Way, the Truth and the Life."

And again, after reading a complex dissertation on a point of theology, she exclaimed: "I don't understand all these arguments. I'm only a child who can hardly lisp the first few letters of the alphabet." Of God, she said: "He created us to know Him and to love Him. Few know Him and so few love Him. He is thought of as a Judge and a Master. How few look upon Him as a Father!" That is an echo of St. Thérèse, but it was an attitude which Marie and indeed the whole Martin family had always had. Thérèse drew in this conception of God with the air she breathed.

As mentioned, Marie's life in Carmel was passed in the ranks. No outward distinction came her way, but Thérèse told her: "I see in you what others cannot see, for you know so well how to hide what you are really like that in eternity many people will be astonished." And, in a burst of gratitude, Thérèse, a year after her entry into Carmel, wrote to Marie: "If it weren't for you, perhaps I should not be here." Thérèse could well be right. What there can be no two opinions about is that we owe *The Story of a Soul* to Marie. She herself has recounted the part she played:

"At the beginning of 1895, Thérèse and I, with Mother Agnès of Jesus, were warming ourselves in front of the fire in the recreation room, and Thérèse recalled one or two events of her childhood. Afterwards I said to Mother Agnès, who was then prioress: 'You allow Thérèse to write verses to entertain the community, and yet she writes nothing for us about what she remembers of her life as a little girl. Mark my words, she is an angel who won't stay long on earth and then we shall have lost a lot of fascinating stories.' Our Reverend Mother hesitated at first, but I kept on pressing her and at last she told Thérèse that she would like her to write down the story of her childhood. Obedient to her prioress, Thérèse immediately set to work and gave the first part of the manuscript to Mother Agnès on January 20, 1896. Mother Agnès later persuaded Mother Marie de Gonzague, who had been re-elected prioress, to order Thérèse to write the story of her religious life, that is, the second part of the manuscript. Then, in September, 1896, I asked her to put in writing what I described as "her little doctrine," her little way of confidence and love. This she did and it is the eleventh chapter of the masterpiece of our Saint."

When Marie read this chapter, written by Thérèse in two days during the little free time she had, she told her sister: "Oh! I was very near to tears as I read these lines, for they are not of this earth, but an echo of the Heart of God. Shall I tell you something? You are possessed by God, really *possessed*—as truly as the wicked are possessed by the devil. I only wished that I could be possessed by Jesus as you are, but I love you so much that I rejoice to know you are more favored than I am."

Thérèse replied at once to this note from Marie, telling her that she was sure that God would not have given her the desire to be possessed by His merciful love unless He had this grace awaiting her. Indeed, He had already given it to her, for she longed to be consumed by Him, and He never gives desires that He cannot fulfill. Thérèse ends her letter: "I love you with all the tenderness of the little heart of a *grateful* child."

Thérèse's letter to Marie—the one which became a chapter—is a document it is almost impossible to believe was written by a young woman of twenty-three. It combines the most intense spiritual passion with the most exact theology. Clear thinking and fiery emotion are fused into a superb paean hymning the infinite mercy and love of God. Outside Holy Scripture, there is little that is comparable. That it should come from the hurried pen of a mortally sick young nun is dazzling proof that she was, as Marie said, truly possessed by God.

Marie's entry into Carmel was another heavy blow for Thérèse for, though Pauline had always held the first place in her heart, Marie was deeply loved—"she guided and comforted me . . . she knew all my thoughts and my longing for Carmel. I loved her so much that I felt I couldn't live without her." A short time before she went, Mr. Martin took them all for a short stay in Alençon. A singular episode occurred.

The town had a convent of Poor Clares, those nuns so often supplied with fish by Mr. Martin in the past. Without saying a word to anyone, Léonie walked across the town and joined them. Mr. Martin was embarrassed and Marie angry. Léonie was unable to stand the severity of life with the Poor Clares and she returned to Les Buissonnets in December. But, as Marie entered Carmel on October 15, there were several weeks when Céline and Thérèse were the only girls left at home. As Thérèse said: "Of that big, happy family, only the two youngest children were left. The doves had flown from the nest, and the two who stayed behind wanted to follow them, but their wings were not yet strong enough."

At this time and for some years before, Thérèse was not a particularly attractive child. She was shy and spoke very little. Her uncle and aunt regarded her as an ignorant little thing, kind and gentle and with the best of intentions, but basically clumsy and incompetent. And rarely a day passed without her bursting into tears. She says: "I was far too sensitive and it was really impossible to put up with me. If, without meaning to, I slightly upset someone I loved, I burst into floods of tears instead of mastering myself, and that, of course, made matters worse. And when I had begun to cheer up I wept again for having wept. It was useless to try to persuade me to be sensible and I could not shake off this horrible habit."

All was changed in the first hour of Christmas Day, 1886. The family returned from Midnight Mass. Ever since she was a small child, her shoes had been placed on this day in the chimney-corner and filled with presents. They were there that day. But her father was tired and, as she ran upstairs to take off her hat before opening her presents, she heard him exclaim: "This is all far too babyish for a big girl like Thérèse, and I hope it's for the last time." Céline flew upstairs expecting to find Thérèse sobbing. Her eyes were bright with tears but they were unshed. "Don't go down yet," Céline begged. "You'll be too upset to look at your shoes straightaway."

Thérèse said years afterwards: "Thérèse was not the same. Jesus had transformed her. With dry eyes I ran down, picked up my shoes and, putting them in front of Papa, pulled out all my presents, looking as happy as a queen. Papa laughed and was his cheerful self again. Céline thought she was dreaming. But it was all real. Thérèse had regained for good that strength of mind she had lost when she was four and a half . . . then began the third period of my life, the best of all, the one most full of divine favors . . . love and a spirit of self-forgetfulness took complete possession of my heart and I've been completely happy."

Thérèse now devoted herself, on the human plane, to Céline. They had always been inseparable. Mrs. Martin said it would be impossible to find two children more devoted to each other. When she was six, Thérèse took a piece of notepaper, which she cut, folded and sewed into the form of a booklet. She wrote only one word on each page and then handed the booklet to Céline. It read: "My darling Céline, I love you a lot and you know I do. Goodbye, darling Céline. Your little Thérèse who loves you with all her heart. Thérèse Martin."

Naturally they had their quarrels. When Céline was really annoyed with Thérèse, she would sternly declare: "You are not my little girl anymore. I have finished with you for good." Thérèse wept anguished tears until Céline hugged and forgave her. Years later, Thérèse was able to say: "Céline never made me unhappy. She was a ray of sunshine, comforting and cheering me." When Céline made her First Communion Thérèse was almost as moved as when she made her own: "I believe that I was given great graces on that day, which was one of the happiest of my life."

There was a gap of nearly four years in age between them, and for a long time Thérèse used to pester her in vain, demanding to know all her secret thoughts. Céline always told her she was too young. Pointing to a stool, she would say: "You'll have to grow by the height of that before I shall be able to trust you." Time and time again Thérèse climbed onto the stool alongside Céline and begged her to confide in her, but she was wasting her time. The barrier of age was too great, for at those ages four years made the difference between a girl and a young woman. However, after what Thérèse called her "Christmas conversion," the barrier was swept away. "Now," Thérèse says, "Jesus wanted us to advance together, and so He linked us by ties stronger than blood. We became spiritual sisters."

Céline was the liveliest of the Martin girls, brisk in manner, vigorous in speech, generous and impetuous. During a lesson at school, one of the mistresses, of English origin, spoke of Joan of Arc, not then canonized, as an adventuress. Céline protested furiously and later in the day hurried to the headmistress and said she would complain to her father unless the tactless mistress was spoken to about her unhappy phrase.

She was always ready to challenge anyone who spoke foolishly or slightingly about affairs or people near to her heart. Coming back from the journey she made to Rome with her father and Thérèse, one of their many fellow travellers chatted with the two sisters and congratulated them on being so fortunate as to see Rome and the Pope. But he was unwise enough to speak of Leo XIII as "a feeble old man." Céline burst out: "It's to be hoped, Monsieur, that you reach his age. You will then perhaps have his wisdom and so will not speak thoughtlessly about matters of which you know nothing."

This readiness to leap into the fray stayed with her to the end. A month or two before her death, when she was nearly ninety, she became warmly indignant about the work of a foreign nun who had illustrated a book of spirituality. She thought her drawings debased the Face of Christ and His saints. "I would like to write to this sister and tell her she has been guilty of real sacrilege," she exclaimed. In her prime, a sharp letter would certainly have been sent. As she grew older, she often regretted her impetuosity.

She wondered at but admired the way in which her sister Marie sat quietly during recreation, listening to all kinds of opinion and never intervening: "There she sat in her invalid chair, calm and serene, and I couldn't stop myself from plunging into the discussion and saying bluntly what I thought."

During the ten weeks of her last illness Céline was gay, brave and full of interest in all that was happening to her. At times she grew a little impatient at the slowness of the approach of death, saying one morning: "Well, as they don't seem ready for me in Heaven, I am going to eat," and asked for food. When a sister came to give her an injection, she exclaimed: "Oh, why not let the lamp slowly burn itself out, as I am not in pain and feel so peaceful."

She told her doctors: "The Gospel says that Our Lord

bowed His Head and yielded up His Spirit. I try to bow
my head but, alas, death refuses to come." When the nuns
spoke of the telegrams they had received about her and of
all the inquiries which poured in, she smiled: "That just
shows you with what thanksgiving my death will be
greeted, but I shall still be the one who will be most relieved."

After a day or two of intense suffering, she was joking,
and one of the doctors said to her: "I've never known dying to be so amusing." "Nor I so painful," she replied.
Throughout her long life—she lived to eighty-nine—she
showed a more inquiring and practical (in the handyman
sense of the word) turn of mind then any of her sisters.
She enjoyed such activities as taking apart a faulty sewing
machine, mending it, and putting it together again; she
was an enthusiastic photographer and an equally enthusiastic—though far less able—painter. Her spiritual director declared: "She has enough life in her for four young
women."

As Thérèse grew older, she was given a room of her
own—an attic room which had been Pauline's studio. It
overlooked the garden, and the nearby park could be seen
from its window. She arranged it to suit her own tastes,
with the result, as she says, that it looked like a crowded
bazaar full of pious objects and curiosities along with a
garden and an aviary. On one wall hung a big, black
wooden cross and some drawings. A basket decorated
with muslin and red ribbon held flowers against another
wall. A photograph of Pauline at the age of ten hung
alone on a third wall. A table stood beneath, and on it
was a spacious birdcage whose inhabitants nearly deafened
visitors with their twittering. A white table held her books
and a statue of Our Lady, honored with vases of flowers
and candles. Scattered around were little baskets made of
shells and cardboard boxes. Flowerpots hung outside the
window and there was a stand inside the room for her
favorite flowers. Before the main window stood her
own personal table with a green cover on which she had

a small statue of St. Joseph, an hourglass, a watchcase, an inkstand, and some flower vases.

The room also had a few ramshackle chairs and a doll's cot which had belonged to Pauline. It was in this room that she and Céline spent hours together. "What lovely talks we had every evening," Thérèse says. "Gazing into the distance we saw the pale moon swim slowly up above the trees, bathing a sleeping world in its silver light. The stars glittered in the dark blue of the sky across which the clouds drifted in the evening breeze—it all lifted our souls towards heaven . . . it seems to me that we were granted graces of the kind given to great saints . . . and graces such as those had to bear abundant fruit. To be good became easy and natural to us."

Céline—"the sweet echo of my soul," as Thérèse called her—behaved magnificently when her sister told her, during those long evening hours of talk and meditation, that she wanted to enter Carmel at once. "By then," as Thérèse says, "we were as united as if we shared a single soul. For some months we had lived that kind of blissful life that young girls dream of; everything around us suited us perfectly; we enjoyed the greatest liberty. We were ideally happy. But we had scarcely time to savor this happiness before it had to be abandoned, yet my darling Céline didn't utter a word of complaint."

Céline also wanted to take the Carmelite habit and, as the elder sister, she might have felt entitled to go first, but "once she knew of my difficulties, she acted as if it were her own vocation that was at stake."

Céline herself says: "I helped Thérèse in all the efforts she made to enter Carmel, despite her youth. I felt all her disappointments more than if I myself were suffering them." Once again we see how all worked to serve God's will for Thérèse.

Her father now had to be told of her desire for Carmel, an ordeal from which she shrank. It was some time before she could pluck up enough courage, but at last she decided to speak on Whitsunday, May 29, 1887. She spent the morning praying to the Apostles to inspire her to say the right words, and in the afternoon after vespers she went up to where he was sitting by the well.

"I said nothing but sat by his side. There were tears in my eyes. He looked at me tenderly and put my head on his breast. 'What's the matter with my little queen? Tell me.' He got up, as if to hide his own feelings, and walked slowly up and down, holding me close to him. Sobbing, I told him that I wanted to enter Carmel. He wept, too, but he said nothing to discourage me, merely remarking that I was very young to take such a very serious step. But I pleaded my cause so well that Papa, with his honest, unaffected nature, was quickly convinced that my desire was inspired by God and, moved by his profound faith, he cried that the Lord did him great honor by asking for yet another of his children,"

Thérèse now thought that all her difficulties were over. They were, in fact, just beginning. She could never have overcome them so quickly had it not been for the unflagging support of nearly all her family. Pauline, in particular, showed remarkable skill and energy in the campaign. Thérèse did not act precipitately, nor did she confide in all her relatives. We have letters she wrote to her two cousins, Jeanne and Marie Guérin, in the summer after she had disclosed her vocation to her father, and they are the simple, artless effusions, full of family gossip and jokes, we would expect to find in the correspondence of young girls. Not one hint is contained in them of all that was stirring in Thérèse's soul.

Nor did she hurry to tell her uncle, who was also her guardian. She was always a little afraid of him, although he had never shown her anything but the most loving kindness. He had, though, a general attitude of bluff, genial heartiness very different from the quiet, withdrawn manner of her father. For some time he had known that Thérèse wanted to enter Carmel, and to that he had no objection, but until Thérèse spoke, he was not aware that she wanted to go at once.

Thérèse first broached the matter to him in October.

As she expected, he gave her a most affectionate little lecture, telling her he was sure that she had a genuine vocation. But that was not the point. For a child to enter Carmel would be a real public scandal. She would be the only Carmelite postulant of such an age in the whole of France. Yet if God wished this to happen, He would make His will quite plain. Meanwhile, until He did, she must not think of quitting the world for Carmel until she was seventeen or eighteen and even then, in his view, she would still be far too young.

All this was reported to Pauline and she soon went into action with a letter to Mr. Guérin, saying that his youngest niece was pale and wretched and felt as if she would die of grief because of his unyielding attitude. And every day Thérèse prayed: "My God, you have all power and my uncle always obeys You. So tell him that You want me without delay." The day he got the letter from Pauline, Thérèse went to see him again. He took her into his study, gently teased her for being afraid of him, then said he had prayed a great deal about her and that he now knew that she was "a little flower that God wanted to pick." He would oppose her desire no longer. Thérèse went home on wings.

Before we follow the next steps of Thérèse's journey to Carmel, let us look a little more closely at Mr. Guérin, a man to whom the whole Martin family owed so much. It was he who persuaded Mr. Martin to settle with his family in Lisieux and rarely can a change of residence have had such momentous results. He was born in 1841, a January child like Thérèse.

He spent several years studying pharmacy in Paris, where what has been described as his "turbulent behavior" caused his relatives a good deal of uneasiness. They were, it is true, relatives who were easily disturbed and yet one feels that, where young Isidore was concerned, their fears were not unjustified. There was, for example, the time when he became involved in an ugly brawl and only managed to emerge unscathed by the use of his sword.

His elder sister wrote him letter after letter from her convent at Le Mans, urging him to mend his ways and accusing him of "taking to wickedness like a duck to water." These were the words of a pious nun who found it impossible to distinguish between thoughtless high spirits and real evil. Isidore reacted as we might expect: for months at a time he ignored his sister and replied to none of her letters. His other sister—the mother of Thérèse— never failed to trust him. Her letters gave him friendly warnings about the moral dangers of life in the capital, but never assumed the tone of a prophet denouncing a dweller in the cities of the plain.

He duly qualified as a pharmacist, went to Lisieux, married a daughter of the proprietor of the main pharmacy in the town, and took over the business. His youthful indiscretions were put behind him: he became a father, one of the most respected citizens of the town and a devout and active Christian.

He and his wife had three children: Jeanne, who married a doctor; Marie, who entered Carmel and was one of Thérèse's novices; and Paul, who died at birth. When he was forty-seven, he inherited a considerable fortune and a château in the countryside near Lisieux. Within four months he sold his pharmacy and in the following year— 1889—he bought a splendid house in the town and, until he died at the age of sixty-eight, devoted his life to work for the Church and the practice of a very active charity.

Towards the end of last century, rationalism and a virulent anti-clericism spread rapidly through France and it was then that education in the country became thoroughly secularized. Mr. Guérin saw that schools and the press were vital weapons that could be used either for or against the Church. As we have seen, Céline persuaded him to take control of a local Catholic newspaper. *Le Normand* came out twice a week and, in a single year, Mr. Guérin wrote seventy-four long polemical articles for it. Thérèse speaks of his "admirable pages which must save souls and make the demons tremble." For five years he directed the paper and wrote for it, and until he died he was always ready to help it with advice and money.

He played a very considerable part in supporting Catholic education in Lisieux, buying a building to convert into a girls' school and giving generous patronage to a Salesian school for boys.

His charity was unstinted when it was the Carmel which was in financial difficulty. And it always was. There were many times when it had no money with which to buy food. Word was sent to Mr. Guérin and relief came at once. At the end of every year the Carmel invariably found that its essential expenses were much greater than its income. For many years Mr. Guérin, quite apart from his frequent but irregular gifts, shouldered this financial burden. He often had to find more than a thousand dollars a year. And it was Mr. Guérin who paid for the printing of Thérèse's autobiography.

He hated destroying letters or documents of any kind, and it is to this that we owe the preservation of so many letters written by Mrs. Martin and much of our detailed knowledge of their family life. Without him, the Carmel of Lisieux, a fairly new foundation, might not have survived long enough to launch the process leading to Thérèse's canonization, and indeed Thérèse's manuscript might not have been published.

Chapter 7

THE EFFORT TO ENTER CARMEL

To return to Thérèse's assault upon Carmel. It seemed that the major obstacles had been overcome: her father, her uncle and the prioress of Carmel were all willing for her to enter. Marie, alone among her sisters, disapproved. Long afterwards, she said: "I strongly and stubbornly resisted her entry at that time because she was far too young, and I knew what terrible grief it would inflict on our father, for Thérèse was the sunshine of his life." But Marie had no power to veto her entrance.

There was, though, one person who had, and he exercised it without hesitation. As soon as the proposal that she should become a postulant was put to him, Canon Delatroëtte, the Superior of Carmel, emphatically turned it down. Under continual badgering by Carmel, he lost his temper and burst out with: "I hear nothing but the name of this girl. One would think the whole future of the convent hung on the admission of this child. But the world won't end because of her, and she must stay with her father until she's the proper age. And don't think that I'm making this stand without having prayed to God for guidance. I refuse to hear any more about it."

Undismayed by the reports they heard of this outburst, Mr. Martin, Thérèse and Céline visited the canon. They got an extremely cold reception, and he remained unmoved by the pleas of both Thérèse and her father, saying that she could live like a Carmelite at home, and so she would lose nothing by having to wait. He did, however, end the interview by pointing out that he was only the representative of the Bishop and that if he were willing to allow her to enter Carmel, he himself neither could nor would have anything more to say. Mr. Martin, hearing this, felt he should perhaps see the Bishop, and his mind was definitely made up by a letter from Pauline telling him of a talk she had had with the chaplain of Carmel.

He was convinced that Mr. Martin should go to Bayeux and put Thérèse's case before the Bishop without a moment's delay, for as a chaplain with much experience, he fully realized that God was free to call souls to a life in religion at whatever age He may choose. Pauline added her own plea: it was essential for him to go to Bayeux unless he wanted Thérèse to be unhappy throughout the projected visit to Italy. "Go and fear nothing," she declared. Once more, Pauline had intervened decisively to serve her sister's purpose.

Thérèse and her father went to Bayeux on October 31. She put her hair up for the first time to try to appear older. They were greeted kindly by the Bishop and his Vicar-General, Father Révérony. Again Mr. Martin and Thérèse spoke as eloquently as they could and Thérèse wept, but all the Bishop would say was that, before he reached a decision, he would consult Canon Delatroëtte. "No reply could have upset me more," says Thérèse. But there was nothing more to be said to the Bishop, although Mr. Martin told him that, having failed to get his permission, Thérèse would ask the Pope for his.

Mr. Martin, Céline and Thérèse departed for Rome, leaving Lisieux at three o'clock on the morning of November 4. They were part of a pilgrimage numbering one hundred ninety-seven people going to Rome to pay homage to Leo XIII, then celebrating the golden jubilee of his priesthood. Thérèse has described her journey through Italy in her autobiography, but we will look again at the culmination of her travels: her meeting with the Pope.

Although her father had told the Bishop of Bayeux that Thérèse would try to get the Pope's consent, it was not at all certain that she would venture to speak to the Holy

Father. The audience Leo XIII gave the French pilgrims took place on November 20. Ten days earlier, Pauline had sent a letter to Thérèse. She said: "I told you not to ask anything from the Holy Father, but today our Mother Prioress and Mother Geneviève [a former prioress and the founder of Lisieux Carmel] say you should, provided you still want to. Don't be afraid and take no notice of the people around you. What if they do hear you? It doesn't matter at all. Ask Jesus what you should say. He will tell you, for it is for love of Him that you will be speaking . . . speak and fear nothing. I have thought over what I am now telling you. Mother Geneviève said to me yesterday: 'Whatever you do, do not forbid her to speak to the Holy Father.' And our Mother Prioress thinks the same . . . be brave and, above all, don't be put off by a first refusal. If the Holy Father rejects your plea, reply: 'O most Holy Father, you cannot refuse me for you know that Our Lord said: 'Suffer little children to come unto Me.' "

"Thérèse wrote back to her at once: "I can't wait to thank you for all you do for me . . Oh Pauline, go on protecting me. I am so far away from you!" The same day, she sent a letter to her aunt and declared that she was determined to speak to the Pope: "I had thought to do it before Pauline wrote to me, but I told myself that if God wanted me to, He would be sure to let me know." She saw Pauline's letter as an expression of God's will.

On the appointed morning the pilgrims heard the Pope say Mass. A Mass of thanksgiving followed and then the audience began. Clothed in white, the Pope sat in a large armchair with a semicircle of prelates behind him. The pilgrims were to advance to him one by one, kneel, kiss his slipper and his hand, receive his blessing, rise and go.

Before the ceremony started, Father Révérony, who accompanied the pilgrimage and had not by any means forgotten Thérèse's interview with his bishop, told everyone that it was strictly forbidden to speak to the Pope. As she heard this warning, Thérèse glanced questioningly at Céline, who uttered one quick, whispered word: "Speak!" When she was asked about this incident many years later,

Céline said: "On such occasions I have only one principle: to do exactly what you have decided to do before-
hand."

When her turn came, Thérèse knelt before the Pope
and kissed his slipper. When he offered her his hand, she
clasped it between hers and, with tears in her eyes, looked
up at him and said: "Most Holy Father, I have a great fa-
vor to ask of you." Thérèse continues the story: "He
leaned forward until his face almost touched mine. His
dark eyes seemed to pierce my soul. 'Most Holy Father,' I
said, 'in honor of your jubilee, let me enter Carmel at fifteen.' My voice trembled, and the Holy Father turned to
Father Révérony, who stared at me with astonished irritation, and said: 'I don't quite understand.' If God had
wanted it, it would have been easy for Father Révérony
to get me what I longed for, but He meant me to have the
cross instead of comfort. "Most Holy Father,' the Vicar-
General told him, 'she is a *child* who wants to enter Carmel at fifteen. The matter is being looked into now by its
superiors.' 'Then, my child,' said the Pope, looking at me
kindly, 'do what the superiors tell you.' I put my hands on
his knees in a last effort and beseeched him: 'Oh! Most
Holy Father, if you said yes, it would be all right with everyone else!' He gazed at me and said very slowly and
distinctly: 'Come, come. You will enter if it is God's
will.' " Thérèse tried to speak again, and she had to be
more or less forcibly removed from the audience cham-
ber.

That evening Thérèse wrote to Pauline: "I cannot tell
you what I felt. It was as if I were annihilated. I felt as
though I'd been abandoned." Marie sent Thérèse a letter
to console her: "You know what the Holy Father said to
you: 'You will enter if it is God's will.' It is just as if God
told you: 'My child, if I want you, you will enter; you will
enter, if I want you, despite all the obstacles and all the
refusals; if I choose, every heart will be changed over-
night, for I hold them all in My hands.' No, Thérèse,
there's nothing to be afraid of." She went on to say that,
so far, she had not paid much attention to Thérèse's

desire to enter Carmel at so early an age, but that now she was sure it was God's will and, of course, His will would be done.

So Marie's objection had died away. And Father Révérony's attitude began to change. Thérèse's behavior before the Pope had shocked him at the time, but he could not remain unimpressed by her courage and determination. Mr. Martin stayed in Rome for two days after the audience, whilst Céline and Thérèse, with most of the pilgrims, went on an excursion to Naples and Pompeii. By chance, he met Father Révérony and spoke to him again with such eloquence about Thérèse that the Vicar-General ended by exclaiming: "Oh well, I'll be at her clothing ceremony if I have to invite myself."

During the whole of the journey back to Lisieux, he went out of his way to be charming to Thérèse, and towards the end, he asked her: "What are you going to do when we get to Lisieux?" She blushed: "I shall go to see my sisters in Carmel." "Well," he declared, "I shall do what I can. Yes, I promise you, everything I can do I will do."

Thérèse did go at once to the Carmel. Pauline again took over the situation. She ordered her sister to write to the Bishop of Bayeux and to Father Révérony. Thérèse wrote the letters and showed them to her uncle. He rewrote the one to the Bishop, saying that the original was too childish. It is much better than his, but Thérèse's relatives were always eager to tarnish the crisp simplicity of her style. These letters were not posted until a few days before Christmas—again at the suggestion of Pauline.

From the moment Thérèse had made known that she wanted to be a Carmelite postulant at once, she had fixed in her own mind Christmas Day as the day on which she would begin her new life and so, after the two letters had gone, she and her father hurried to the post office each day after Mass to see if the Bishop's permission had arrived. They were always disappointed. Christmas came, but the Bishop was silent and she went sadly to midnight Mass.

On her return home she found in her room a bowl of water in which a little model boat was floating. In it was an image of the Child Jesus with a tiny ball at His side. On the sail, in Céline's handwriting, were the words: "I sleep, but My Heart keeps watch." The word "Resignation" was on the boat. Thérèse had often said she wished to be like a toy ball to the Child Jesus, something without any personal will, something He could use exactly as He wished.

On the afternoon of Christmas day, Thérèse had a fit of weeping and then went to visit the Carmelites. The grill was opened, and as she saw a statue of the Child Jesus holding in His hand a ball inscribed with her name, the nuns sang a poem written for her by Pauline. She wept again, but her tears were tears of happiness.

On New Year's Day she was told that a letter from the Bishop authorizing her entry had arrived at the Carmel on December 28, Holy Innocents' Day, but even this news had its bitterness, for the prioress decided that she was not to be admitted before Lent. There were two reasons for this: Mother Marie de Gonzague hoped this delay of three months might go some way towards placating Canon Delatroëtte, and she thought that it would be unfair to Thérèse to make her face the severity of a Carmelite Lent before she had had sufficient time to become accustomed to the Rule.

It was Thérèse's final disappointment, but it was a sharp one. However, she used this last period of waiting in trying to live with greater detachment and mortification. The three months went quickly and at last the moment arrived for which she had so passionately longed. On Monday, April 6, 1888, the door of Carmel closed behind her.

The redoubtable Canon Delatroëtte said, as she stepped over the threshold: "Reverend Mother, sing a *Te Deum*. It is at the order of His Lordship the Bishop that I give you this fifteen-year-old child whose entrance you have desired. I hope you will not be disappointed in her, but I want you to bear in mind that you and you alone bear the responsibility if things do not turn out as you expect."

Chapter 8

THE CARMEL OF LISIEUX—
SISTER THERESE

The Carmel of Lisieux was a strange place, and one can easily imagine the forthright language with which St. Teresa of Jesus, the Mother of Carmel, would have castigated the way of life within its walls. It was not an old foundation. Fifty years, almost to the day, before Thérèse became a postulant, two nuns and four novices came to Lisieux to establish a Carmel there. A year or two before that, two young sisters named Gosselin had wished to become Carmelites but were rejected because their health was not thought good enough. They were not without money and decided to use it to found a Carmel where, as benefactors, they could live under special vows—a practice which the Order permits. Their idea was put before the Bishop of Bayeux and he approved of it on condition that the Carmel was set up in Lisieux. A priest of the town was made its superior, and his first task was to find a Carmel which would release some nuns to start the new community. It was not an easy one, but after more than a year his prayers were answered, and the Carmel of Poitiers offered to lend him two nuns, stipulating only that the Gosselin girls and two others who also wished to become Carmelites should pass their noviciate at Poitiers. This they did.

On March 16, 1838, the two nuns and the four novices arrived in Lisieux. Night was falling and a heavy rain beat on the canvas awning of the rough cart in which they rode. The cart had been lent to them, instead of a carriage, by someone a shade too eager not to offend Carmelite poverty. Their temporary home was the first floor of a thatched house owned by a devout widow. She too displayed excessive reverence for the Carmelite Rule, for learning that silence was never broken in a Carmel after eight o'clock at night, she met them, took them to her house but spoke not one word to them until next morning.

It was a house that could not have been less suitable. There was a courtyard and a garden overlooked by the windows of all the neighboring houses. There were no rooms fit to serve as cells for the novices, and they had to make do with a dormitory constructed out of two attic rooms knocked together. One room was a chapel, another was the choir, and a third (six yards square) had been partitioned into three to form a kitchen, a refectory and recreation room, and a cell for the sub-prioress (on entering or leaving it, she had to take great care to avoid knocking the pots and pans off the stove). The prioress also had a cell to herself. The furnishing matched the accomodation: in the kitchen a packing-case was the sideboard and the larder was formed by a fire screen pushed across a corner. Washing up had to be done in the middle of a meal so that there would be clean crockery for the end of it.

But, as the story of the foundation says: "They knew the joy that comes from privations gladly accepted, and the inconveniences they had to endure added to the gaiety of their talk at recreation. They were full of fervor and led a life as faithful to the Rule as was possible in such a convent."

For five months they stayed there, and then a house was bought in the Rue de Livarot, one much more suitable for their purpose though still far from being wholly satisfactory. There was no accommodation for the laywomen, who at first served as laysisters, and this meant that one of the postulants had to leave the enclosure each evening to secure the outer door and that the community was unable to get in touch with the outside world at night in case of illness or any other kind of trouble. But on September 5, 1838, it became the Carmel of Lisieux. And it was to that Carmel, by then greatly enlarged, that Thérèse went.

I began this chapter by saying it was a strange place. That is not merely my personal opinion. Canon Delatroëtte told the Prioress: "If the state of affairs here were known outside your walls, they'd burn your convent to the ground." The ideal Carmel is a building completely shut off from the world, in which twenty or so women live until they die, spending their time in prayer, work and penance, and in showing exquisite charity to each other. Their food is scanty and their hours of sleep few. Each has a cell, bare and bleak in appearance, containing a bed with a straw pallet for a mattress, a stool and a small table. There is no possibility of enjoying any physical comfort. The very habits they wear are a severe penance in themselves. Such an existence is endurable only because those who chose it wish to concentrate their whole being on contemplating and loving God undisturbed by the distractions of the world. Such is the situation in an ideal Carmelite convent. At Lisieux it was a little different.

The prioress was Mother Marie de Gonzague, formerly Marie Adèle Rosalie Davy de Virville, the daughter of a noble family who entered the Carmel when she was twenty-six. She had been there twenty-eight years when Thérèse arrived. A woman of a strong and passionate nature, she had the potentialities of a great prioress, but she failed to respond to the high demands of her position. She never understood the true, inner significance and purpose of the Carmelite Rule and she never forgot that she was an aristocrat and a highly intelligent and well-educated woman ruling over subjects greatly inferior to her in worldly attributes.

She had no equal in brains and force of personality until Pauline and Marie Martin entered the Carmel. Steps should have been taken early in her conventual life to channel the force of her turbulent nature and direct it aright, for it must soon have been obvious that she was an unusual nun. She became sub-prioress six years after her entry, and she had not held that office for long when she one day disappeared and was not discovered until night, when some of the nuns found her crouching under a ladder in the corner of the garden. She was led to the cell of the prioress and there tried to throw herself out of the window, but was caught in time and held back by a lay-sister. A spasm of jealousy was the cause of that escapade.

Yet she became prioress a few years later, a position she was to hold for twenty-one years. How unsuitable she was to reign in one of the most austere orders of the Church can be seen when we learn that she had a cat which she fed on calf's liver and sugared milk. If the animal caught a bird, she took it away, had it roasted and served to him with sauce. Once the cat was lost and in the evening, during the great silence which may not be broken except for the gravest reason, Mother Marie summoned several nuns and had them hunting up and down the garden, calling for the missing animal.

Until 1891, the prioress of a convent laid down the frequency with which her nuns could receive Holy Communion. After that year, it was a matter for a priest, the superior of the community. The papal decree establishing this was at first accepted with good grace by Mother Marie, but when some nuns were allowed daily Communion, while others were permitted it less frequently, she grew jealous of the priest's authority and succeeded in ensuring that each nun had the same number of Communions. She gravely abused this matter of Holy Communion in other ways, once going so far as promising it to a nun if she succeeded in catching a rat.

She remained too closely attached to her family. Her sister, who was unhappily married and could not get along with her daughter, was a frequent visitor to the Carmel, and it was nothing unusual for her to arrive with her grandchildren and stay for some weeks in the gatehouse of the convent. During her stay, the nuns acted as her servants, even having to mend her underclothes and embroider her coat-of-arms onto her tablecloths and handkerchiefs. The whole community sighed when the arrival of this sister was announced.

Mother Marie lent her sister more than three thousand dollars from the Carmel's scanty capital and, to make matters worse, her sister failed to pay the interest regularly. The nuns complained: "When from time to time a banknote did arrive from the countess, she had to be thanked as if she had sent it as a gift." The community did get back its money when she died, along with thirty dollars as a final bit of interest, but no one knew if more were due, as Mother Marie never troubled to keep accounts.

Discipline among the nuns was lax. During her years as prioress, Mother Marie de Gonzague allowed the parlor to degenerate into something almost like a social club. A friend visited her there every day and supplied her with the latest news and gossip about her friends in the world, and the relatives of the other nuns dropped in once a week and stayed chatting for far longer than the regulation time. And a steady stream of presents came for the nuns from their friends and relatives.

There were just over twenty nuns there when Thérèse entered. She was, of course, by far the youngest. The only other novice was eight years older. Apart from her two sisters, most of the nuns were fifty or more. Four were between sixty and eighty-five. With the exception of the prioress, the novice-mistress, Marie and Pauline, they were all women of the lower-middle or working class and, as entry into a convent does not automatically free one of all the manners and attitudes imposed by one's upbringing, there must have been much to grade upon the sensibilities of the Martin girls. But to Thérèse all was delightful: "My desires were fulfilled at last, and my soul knew a peace too complete to be described, and I have never lost that peace even in the midst of the greatest trials ... Life in the convent was just as I thought it would be, and none of the sacrifices I had to make surprised me."

We have seen how Mother Marie de Gonzague encouraged Thérèse in her longing to enter Carmel at such an early age and how she ignored the opinion of Canon Delatroëtte, yet her attitude to her as a postulant and as a novice must have startled Thérèse. It certainly shocked Pauline. Of Mother Marie, Thérèse declared: "She never met me without finding fault, and I remember that once when I had left a cobweb in the cloister, she said to me before the whole community: 'Our cloister is very obviously swept by a child of fifteen. It's disgraceful. Go off and sweep away the cobweb and be more careful next time' ... When I was a postulant, the novice-mistress used to send me out to weed the garden at half-past four every afternoon. I nearly always ran into Mother Marie de Gonzague. On one occasion, she exclaimed: 'Really, child, you do absolutely nothing. What is one to think of a postulant who has to be sent out for a walk every day?' "

The novice-mistress gave Thérèse orders to tell her whenever she had a stomach ache. Perhaps the convent food was upsetting Thérèse but, whatever the cause, she had pains in her stomach every day and faithfully, but with great embarrassment, reported this to the novice-mistress, who became convinced that Thérèse's health was not good enough to endure the asceticism imposed by the Rule. After every report from Thérèse, she went to Mother Marie and asked for some medicine for her. The prioress, who was never ill, had little sympathy for the sick and often said: "Nowadays, people have illnesses that were never heard of before, and it's a sin to nurse them."

Looking forward a few years to the last days of Thérèse, when she lay dying in extreme agony, we may note that Mother Marie refused to allow the doctor to give her injections of morphine. This was not because of any ill will, any malice towards Thérèse. She had also refused morphine to Mother Geneviève, the foundress of the Carmel, when she was dying, believing that no Carmelite should escape suffering. So in the matter of Thérèse's stomach aches she showed only irritation: "The child never stops complaining. We are here in Carmel to suffer, so if she cannot endure the life she's no business to be here."

Pauline was greatly upset at the behavior of Mother Marie towards her sister and ventured to speak to her about it. She was quickly and sharply put in her place. "Now we see just what happens when two sisters are together in one convent," Mother Marie told her. "Naturally you want to see Sister Thérèse pushed forward and given special treatment. That would be quite the wrong course, for her pride is far greater than you think. She needs to be constantly humiliated. And as for her health, well that is no business of yours. We shall do what we think fit."

On a first reading, these words of the prioress merely seem to confirm her eccentricity. "Thérèse proud? Surely it is not possible seriously to accuse her of such a sin, and yet, and yet . . . we remember that Mrs. Martin told of how, teasing her, she one day said: "Thérèse, if you will kiss the ground, I will give you a penny." This seemed quite a lot of money to the little girl, but she drew herself up and replied: "No thank you, Mamma, I would rather go without the penny." We remember, too, that her confessor told her that she could easily have become a little demon. She had a will of iron. It showed itself in her determination to enter Carmel at the age she did, a determination which nothing ever shook for a moment. Her sisters saw her as a paragon of goodness and, until she had been a nun for some years, still thought of her as a child.

Mother Marie de Gonzague was the first to realize the true quality of her soul. At the time when she was governing her with a heavy hand, she was writing to the Guérins: "I never thought it possible that a fifteen year old girl could have such a mature mind. One cannot find fault with her." Later she told a priest: Out of the whole community, Sister Thérèse would be my choice for prioress. She is perfection itself, apart from one fault—her three sisters."

Yet for a long time she dealt severely with Thérèse. It

was, though, a deliberate policy, for it is clear she recognized that, in this young postulant, she had a girl very different in quality from any she had known before. Mother Marie de Gonzague had grave faults and yet, without hesitation, she spotted the potential greatness of Thérèse and equally quickly saw that it was still only potential and that all the superb spiritual qualities of the girl needed to be harshly disciplined if they were to flower as they should. Though her sisters were shocked at the behavior of Mother Marie, Thérèse herself was grateful. She told the prioress: "Jesus was well aware that this little flower needed the life-giving water of humiliation. It was too frail to take root without such watering, and it was by your hands, Mother, that this blessing was dispensed . . . I thank you with all my heart for not having been too gentle with me."

Thérèse recalled that, in her early days in the convent, she rarely met the prioress without having to kiss the ground in penance for some fault she had committed, and it was the same on the few occasions when she went to her for spiritual guidance: "What a priceless grace this was! God Himself was clearly dealing with me through His representative. What should I have become if I had been the spoiled playing of the community—as some people outside thought I was. Perhaps instead of seeing Our Lord acting through my superiors, I might have regarded them only as persons and my heart, so free when I was in the world, might have been caught up in human attachments in the cloister. Happily I was preserved from that misfortune."

I confess that I have great affection for and sympathy with Mother Marie de Gonzague. It is true, as I have made plain, that on very many counts she was far from being an ideal prioress. But she was a character—perhaps a "card" would be the right word—and a good woman. She had a great deal to put up with. At one time, she had under her the four Martin sisters and one of their cousins. They would not, admittedly, have been there without her consent, a fact which in itself shows that she was no fool: she knew virtue when she met it. But I imagine there must have been moments when she felt a little over-whelmed by the Martins, all of whom had strong per-sonalities, which grew no weaker upon entry into Carmel. One has only to look at photographs of Pauline to feel quite sure that no one in Carmel, from the newest novice to the prioress, was ever in doubt as to what she thought or felt. This is not a hostile criticism of Pauline, merely a recognition that she was a woman of very considerable will and ability and determined to exercise both to achieve ends she thought were good.

We must not equate virtue with meekness. Nor must we believe that women cease to have human failings the moment they put on the habit of Carmel: they are in Car-mel because they want to overcome them, but they sel-dom succeed completely. So it would not be surprising if there were some brisk exchanges between Mother Marie and Mother Agnès, particularly in view of the fact that each of them knew there was every likelihood that one might succeed the other as prioress at the end of each three years. And Mother Marie must have known that Pauline herself, two of her sisters—and even Thérèse—together with Marie Guérin would all feel that Pauline was the right and proper person to assume command. In other words, she knew that there was always nearly twenty-five percent of the community who were sure that she should be replaced by Pauline. They would do all in their power not to show this, but only a fool would be unaware of what they felt, and as I have said, Mother Marie de Gonzague was no fool.

It is instructive to look at the photographs of the Carmel nuns taken by Céline. Three people stand out: Thérèse, Pauline and Mother Marie de Gonzague. Know-ing the future of Thérèse it is hard to come to her fresh. We recognize her at once and know that she is *Saint* Thérèse, yet I feel that someone who had neither heard of her nor seen her picture would notice her in these group photographs. There is a striking difference between the expression on her face and that on those of her companions. It is hard to define, but it is there. As for Pauline—well, it is a face not easily forgotten and one, most emphatically, of a woman with whom a person would not care to clash. There are photographs of Thérèse where she is smiling with mouth and eyes. Pauline's eyes do not smile. Thérèse's eyes are clear and steady, but they are often looking beyond this world. The gaze of Pauline misses nothing. She is obviously fully aware of everything that is happening around her, but she sees no deeper than the camera lens she faces.

Then we have Mother Marie de Gonzague. She has a strange, weather-beaten face, and there is nearly always the suspicion of a smile, a cynically tolerant smile—a very kindly one though. The cynicism is not bitter, but the kind which renders its possessor incapable of being surprised at any human antics. In one or two photographs, she looks bored and succeeds in achieving complete detachment from the group. Looking at her, it becomes easy to understand why, in spite of the vagaries of her behavior, she never lost the love of her nuns.

Much may be pardoned a woman who so quickly realized the greatness of Thérèse. It is easy to be wise after a canonization. We all can then say: "Of course, she was a saint. It was always obvious." But Mother Marie knew in the first month or two of Thérèse's postulancy that she was handling someone extraordinary, someone who moved on quite a different plane from anyone she had known. After her death, Mother Marie wrote in the Carmel's register: "The nine and a half years she spent among us leave our souls fragrant with the most beautiful virtues with which the life of a Carmelite can be filled. A perfect model of humility, obedience, charity, prudence, detachment and regularity, she fulfilled the difficult discipline of mistress of novices with a sagacity and affection which nothing could equal, save her love for God. This angel of earth had the happiness of taking flight to her Beloved in an act of love. Oh, dear loved one, watch over your Carmel." From first to last, she never had the slightest doubt about the quality of Thérèse. For that we must always be grateful. As for her faults, they were venial and must long ago have been forgiven.

She died of cancer of the tongue seven years after Thérèse. As she lay dying, she said to Mother Agnès, then prioress: "No one in this house has been as guilty as I. Yet I trust in God and in my little Thérèse. She will intercede for me and win my salvation." During Thérèse's life, Mother Agnès had replaced Mother Marie as prioress for three years. Those years had been troubled ones, for Mother Marie had not taken kindly to being under the authority of the younger woman and had tried to split the nuns into factions, and, as we have seen, Mother Agnès could never become reconciled to Mother Marie's treatment of Thérèse. Yet as Mother Marie drew near death, the two women put aside their differences. Mother Agnès says: "She turned more and more to me. She loved me and I her. And I was grateful to her, because it was owing to her domination of the nuns and even of the superior that we four sisters were in the same Carmel, together with our cousin. All five of us were with her during her last night on earth."

The great sign of Mother Marie's complete trust in Thérèse came when she made Thérèse novice-mistress—in fact, though not with the title. Mother Agnès became prioress in 1893, replacing Mother Marie, who was given the office of novice-mistress. Mother Agnès knew that Mother Marie was eminently unsuited to her new task, but she says: "I felt I had to appoint her in order to avoid a greater evil. But to try to lessen the mischief she might cause, I assigned Thérèse to supervise her two companions, but in reality I was relying on her to guide the novices." So for three years Thérèse had the almost impossible task of instructing the novices without Mother Marie's knowledge, although Mother Marie was the titular novice-mistress.

Years later, these novices, then fully professed nuns, said they all understood that, during this period, they had to follow the intructions of Thérèse as "unobtrusively and tactfully" as possibly "so as not to rouse Mother Marie's jealousy nor openly flout her authority." It is not conceivable that this deplorable state of affairs escaped Mother Marie's notice, and one would have thought that when she became prioress again in 1896, she would at once have ended the irregularity of the situation in which Thérèse had been placed. But no. It is true she did retain for herself the office of novice-mistress, but she called Thérèse the senior novice, and for nearly two years, until she became too ill to work, Thérèse, with the full approval and support of Mother Marie de Gonzague, was responsible for training the novices. It was invaluable training for Thérèse herself.

Here we must look for a moment at Mother Geneviève de Saint-Thérèse who, at the time of Thérèse's entry into Carmel, was a nun of eighty-three and a most venerated figure there, for she was one of the two nuns who went from Poitiers to Lisieux to found the convent, and it was she who was regarded as the foundress. She was ill and died just over two years after the arrival of Thérèse, whose entry she had warmly supported. A great gulf of years lay between them, and there were times when the aged, ailing woman was startled by what seemed to her the rashness and boldness of some of the young girl's thoughts and aspirations. Yet she had an influence on Thérèse out of all proportion to the times they spent together and the words they exchanged. Thérèse says that more than once she had received great spiritual favors through her. She used to visit her on Sundays.

One day, when she arrived, she found two nuns there and turned away to leave as not more than two visitors were allowed at a time. Mother Geneviève called to her: "Just a moment, my child, I've a little something to tell you. Whenever you come, you ask me to give you a spiritual bouquet. So now today I give you this one: serve God in peace and with joy. Remember, my child, that our God is the God of peace."

Thérèse was present when she died, and she noticed a

tear glistening on her eyelash. It was still there when she was laid out in the choir, and in the evening Thérèse crept in and wiped it away with a tiny scrap of linen which she placed in the little locket which held her vows. Some nights afterwards, Thérèse dreamt she was watching Mother Geneviève make her will. She left something to every nun but when it came to Thérèse's turn there was nothing left. Mother Geneviève raised herself up in bed and very clearly repeated three times the words: "To, you, I leave my heart." In three matters she influenced Thérèse.

On the question of penance, Thérèse had very definite views which were at variance with much of the spirituality of her time. She spoke to Mother Agnès and to Cèline about them. Cèline reports: "She said she had noticed that the nuns most given to savage penitential exercises were by no means the most perfect. Self-love seemed to feed on excessive bodily penance. And such penance counted as absolutely nothing alongside charity." At the beginning of her life in religion, Mother Agnès was strongly inclined to penance over and above that enjoined in the Rule. She spoke to Thérèse, not long before she died, about using instruments of penance. Thérèse told her to be very careful and declared that such mortifications were not meant for those who followed her "Little Way." She quoted the words of Our Lord: "Take my yoke upon yourselves, and learn from me; I am gentle and humble of heart; and you shall find rest for your souls. For my yoke is easy and my burden is light," and she went on: "You see, Mother, we have to take *His* yoke. He does not tell us to burden ourselves with another."

By the yoke of Our Lord she meant not only the normal spiritual and physical trials of community life, but complete obedience to the Carmelite Rule. Now Mother Geneviève was once asked by Mother Marie de Gonzague about the kind of mortification novices should be allowed to practice over and above those enjoined by the Rule. She at once said: "Be very careful. Without the greatest prudence and very sound judgment, all extra mortification is vanity and nourishes self-love. Teach your novices to break their will, to practice charity and to give complete obedience to the Rule. That is the true and solid penance which is always pleasing to God." She was, of course, speaking in the old tradition of Carmel, for St. John of the Cross speaks of "the spiritual gluttons who kill themselves with penances, attracted by the pleasure they find in them," and he condemned them as "imperfect and devoid of reason, for they set bodily penance before subjection and obedience, which is penance of the reason and therefore a sacrifice more acceptable and pleasing to God than any other."

Mère Geneviève was also instrumental and introducing into the Lisieux Carmel the devotion to the Holy Face of Our Lord. This devotion was not a new one. It goes back to the very ancient tradition which says that when Our Lord was carrying His Cross to Calvary a woman named Veronica burst from the crowd of spectators lining the street and held out to Him the veil from her head to wipe the blood and the sweat from His Face. He used it and handed it back to her. The veil bore the imprint of His Face. That is the tradition, and it is a fact that a veil with the outline of the Holy Face was publicly venerated in Rome in the year 610.

In France, in the Carmel of Tours, was a nun, Sister Marie de St. Pierre, who revived this devotion which, although never dead, had long been dormant. In 1845 she declared that she had been told by Our Lord that He would afford great graces to those who gave to His Face the honor and devotion due to it. In Tours there lived at that time Mr. Léon Dupont, known after his death as the "Holy Man of Tours." News of Our Lord's revelation to Sister Marie reached him and he seized upon it and, as the years passed, became the servant of the Holy Face with such single-minded devotion that the cult spread throughout France and much of the rest of western Europe. The cause of his beatification has been officially introduced.

A Confraternity of the Holy Face was established in Tours and in 1885 Mr. Martin and four of his daughters became members. In the Confraternity's list of members, one can still read the entry: "Le 26 avril, No. 7382, Madamoiselle Thérèse Martin." Pauline had entered Carmel nearly three years earlier and had there been made fully aware of this devotion. For, two years after the nun of the Tours Carmel had spoken, Mother Geneviève learned of her message and was deeply moved by it. It was not long before she gained permission from the Bishop to place reproduction of Veronica's veil in the convent chapel. Without her devotion to the Holy Face, it is highly improbable that Pauline would have been swept into this current of love for this manifestation of Our Lord's humanity and, if she had not been, it would not have become the center of Thérèse's spiritual life.

Thérèse says: "It is through you, Pauline, that I became aware of the richness of the treasures hidden in the Holy Face. You were the first of us to enter Carmel and you were equally the first of us to understand the mysteries of love which are hidden in the Face of Our Lord, Then you called me to you and I also understood. I understood what true glory was. He whose kingdom is not of this world showed me that true wisdom was 'to seek to be unknown and to be esteemed as nothing' and 'to rejoice in despising myself.' I longed for my face to be like that of Jesus, truly hidden so that it could be recognized by no one. I wanted only to suffer and to be forgotten."

When Thérèse became a postulant, she was given the name of Thérèse of the Child Jesus. At her clothing, she was granted permission to change it to Thérèse of the Child Jesus of the Holy Face. She sought this permission because she was so deeply moved by the fate of her father, a fate which reminded her of the suffering and humiliation of Jesus during His Passion. Mr. Martin was cruelly afflicted during the last years of his life. He had a very slight stroke just before the journey to Rome with Céline and Thérèse. It was the first sign of a physical and mental deterioration which finally paralyzed him and reduced him to the state of an imbecile. Before he fully lost the use of his reason, he was aware of his humiliating condition and used to pull a sheet or any bit of cloth over his face to hide himself from the gaze of others.

Years before, Mr. Martin had gone away from Les Buissonnets for a few days. In the middle of one afternoon during his absence Thérèse, standing at a window looking across the garden, saw a man walk past the washhouse. He was dressed like her father and was of the same height. She could not see his face, for it was hidden by a thick veil. She shouted to him, but the figure took no notice and walked through a little group of trees. She watched to see him come out beyond them, but he never appeared. Marie and Pauline were in the next room. Marie ran to Thérèse when she heard her shout, and Thérèse told her what she had seen. The maid was questioned, but she had not left the kitchen. The sisters went into the garden and searched it, but they found no trace of the mysterious visitor.

When Mr. Martin began his sufferings, Thérèse was sure she had had a prophetic vision, and as she thought of her father, whose illness disfigured his face, the tortured Face of Our Lord took on a new meaning for her. Her father, a man of saintly life, had suddenly been destroyed as a sentient human being, and yet she knew that by any natural standard of judgment no man so little deserved such an ending to his life. As I have said, it brought home to her the full enormity and horror of Our Lord's Passion and death. She realized with all her being that His abasement was the price of our salvation and that the abasement of oneself, the willing abandonment of all human pretensions was the essential step—or rather, the long and painful journey necessary for all who sought to love God.

She meditated ceaselessly on the fifty-third chapter of Isaias: "There is no beauty in him, nor comeliness: and we have seen him, and there was no sightliness, that we should be desirous of him: Despised, and the most abject of men, a man of sorrows, and acquainted with infirmity: and his look *was* as it were hidden and despised, whereupon we esteemed him not. Surely he hath borne our infirmities and carried our sorrows: and we have thought him as our iniquities, he was bruised for our sins; the chastisement of our peace *was* upon him, and by his bruises we are healed."

"On these words of Isaias," she says, "I have based the whole of my devotion to the Holy Face, or rather they are the foundation on which all my devotion rests." And Mother Agnès could declare: "She was tenderly devoted to the Child Jesus, but this devotion could not be compared to her feeling for the Holy Face;" and Céline said: "This devotion was the crown, the full blossoming of her love for the sacred Humanity of Jesus. The Holy Face was the mirror in which she saw the Soul and the Heart of her Beloved . . . It was from gazing at the wounded Face of Jesus and thinking of Its humiliation that she learned humility and the love of suffering, that she became so eager to sacrifice herself and eager to win souls for God. From it she learned detachment from creatures and drew the strength to practice all her virtues." On the Feast of the Transfiguration, a few weeks before she died, a picture of the Holy Face was placed on her bedside table. She exclaimed: "What a good thing it was that Our Lord closed His eyes before giving us His portrait. For as the eyes are the mirror of the soul, we should die of joy if we could see His soul."

Céline, after she became a Carmelite, served the cult of the Holy Face with her brush. In 1898, the Holy Shroud of Turin was taken from its leaden case and displayed for public veneration. Many pilgrimages were made to this precious relic, and a small library of books was produced about it. Mr. Guérin bought one of these books, profusely illustrated with photographs of the Shroud, and gave it to Céline. The impressions on the Shroud were like a film negative; photographs of them turned the negative into a print. In her cell, Céline studied them and was profoundly stirred. She cried: "This is indeed my Jesus as my heart knows Him," and there and then she decided to produce a picture of the Holy Face from the image on the Shroud.

She began work at Easter in 1904 and made a charcoal drawing, but she was told it would not reproduce well, so the next year she tried again, this time using paint. Every moment of her spare time was given up to the task and every evening she laid her brushes and canvas at the foot of that statue of Our Lady by which Thérèse had been healed. The picture won the Grand Prix at an international exhibition of religious art held in Holland in 1909. Today, uncounted millions of copies of it exist, and it has become the universally accepted representation of the Holy Face.

Great pleasure and consolation are to be gained in discovering the secret working of God, in seeing apparently unrelated people and events quietly being brought together to form a significant picture from scattered jigsaw pieces, in watching a pattern evolve from separate broken, multi-colored threads. I have been in the parlors of many Carmels, but the one I remember best is the high, white room in the Carmel of Tours where I held in my hand the heart of Sister Marie de St. Pierre. Small, dark, mummified, it had, more than a hundred years before, raced with excited awe as she heard Our Lord speak of His Holy Face, and, as I gazed at it, I saw a young nun setting out to found a Carmel in Lisieux, the tall figure of Mr. Dupont healing people with oil from the lamp which always burned beneath his picture of the Holy Face, a veiled phantom walking across a sunlit garden, a paralyzed old man with the empty eyes and vacant face of the insane—all images without meaning until they suddenly rushed together and coalesced to produce the mainspring of the spirituality of the greatest saint of our time.

As we know, Thérèse was, to all intents and purposes, the novice-mistress for nearly five years. When Mother Geneviève was a nun at Poitiers, she was appointed novice-mistress. The Bishop of Orléans, hearing of this, wrote to her about her new position. His words were: "It is of great importance. What you must do first of all is to beseech God to bless your work. Then, that done, you must be so kindly disposed towards your novices that you win their confidence and their hearts. And you must exercise great skill in reading their character and discovering what goes on in the depth of their souls. You must be gentle and never show impatience, listening to everything without giving any sign of being upset. In all your dealings, show equability and humility. With these young girls, you must start by giving them a real desire to belong to God and to offer Him everything. Once you can do this, the rest will come much more easily. Give them great confidence in God and, above all, emphasize that He is not a quarrelsome God. He gladly forgives those souls who love Him. To teach your novices to rid themselves of their defects, train them to start by making trifling sacrifices— spiritual ones above all—and, at first, let them be so small that they are hardly any effort. Destroy their self-love. When they commit a fault, console them and promise to pray for them. See that they are frank and brief with their confessor. Tell them to despise temptation. Be astonished at nothing or discouraged by anything and never seek consolation from them."

Mother Geneviève never destroyed this letter, and it guided her in all her dealings with her novices. Mother Agnès was very close to her during her last years, so close that Thérèse could tell her: "The spirit of Mother Geneviève dwells in you quite unchanged," and it can be taken that she knew the contents of this letter and how they had been used to school a succession of novices. It is most unlikely that she did not pass on to Thérèse the Bishop's instructions when she asked her to act as unofficial novice-mistress. Certainly, Thérèse's methods were his.

"During all the time I've spent with the novices, my life has been one of war and struggle. God has worked for me and I have worked for Him. My soul has never made such progress." That is what Thérèse says. It was a crucial period in her development, crucial too for us, for without it we should know far, far less about her. It is, indeed, possible that we should know nothing, for she might have had very little to say.

To train her novices, she had to put into words what she thought, and she had also to think more profoundly than if she were dealing only with her own soul. The novices disclosed some of the vagaries of human nature to her and she had, of course, to fight these by talking to their victims, by praying for them, and by making an ever sharpening sacrifice of herself. She grew into a deeper knowledge of human weakness and a richer awareness of God's merciful love. Towards the end of her autobiography she wrote about her discoveries; she also spoke about them to her sisters and they jotted down her words. We can say quite confidently that three-quarters of the words of Thérèse would have been lost forever but for her years with the novices.

Some of these novices were not very prepossessing: Céline was one of them and so was Marie Guérin, Thérèse's cousin. These two naturally had their imperfections but, to say the least, they had a rough idea of what Thérèse was talking about. But one of the novices—a lay-sister—had been a maidservant, had suffered ill-treatment, and had known the utmost poverty. She was frightened of Thérèse and ran away and hid herself whenever she was to go to Thérèse's cell for instruction. Thérèse patiently hunted her down each time and tried to talk away her fear. Another novice was simply stupid and had the greatest difficulty in understanding Thérèse's simplest words. A third, too, was not very talented and seemed to have no real vocation for Carmel. The five novices, taken together, offered their mistress a fairly comprehensive collection of human imperfections: vanity, immaturity, obstinacy, willfulness, pettiness, cowardice—the list is endless. Yet they remained in Carmel and died there as good Carmelites.

Thérèse says that when she was asked to train the novices she instantly realized that the task was quite beyond her: "So I flung myself into the arms of God like a little child and, hiding my face against Him, said: 'Lord, I am far too small to feed your children. If You want me to give each one what she needs, You will have to fill my hand and then, without leaving Your arms or even turning my head, I will give Your treasures to every one of them who comes and asks me for food. If she finds it to her taste, I shall know that it is to You and not to me that she is indebted. But if she grumbles and says it is bitter, I shall not worry, but shall do all I can to persuade her that it is food which You have provided, and I shall take good care to seek no other for her.' Once I understood how impossible it was for me to do anything by myself, my task no longer seemed difficult. I felt that the one essential thing was to draw closer and closer to Jesus and that all the rest would be mine without asking. And my trust has never been betrayed. God has always filled my hand whenever I have had to nourish the souls of my sisters."

She gathered the novices around her every day for half-an-hour in the early afternoon, at which time either she herself or one of them read a few passages from the Carmelite Rule or the Constitutions. She would then explain or comment on what had been read. Or perhaps she would answer questions put to her or expound a verse of Scripture. She had no set method for conducting these half-hours. Each novice had to go to her regularly for private instruction. She knew that "every one has to fight more or less the same battles, yet souls differ even more than faces and so they all need different treatment. With some I haven't to be afraid of humbling myself by confessing my own struggles and defeats, for my little sisters then tell me of all their own faults, for they see that I have the same weaknesses and that I understand all about them through my own experience. But with others I have to do exactly the contrary if I am to help them. I must be very firm and never go back on anything I say. To descend to their level then would not be humility, but weakness. God has made me not afraid of a fight and, at whatever cost, I will do my duty. More than once I've been told: 'If you want to influence me, you will have to be sweet and gentle; trying to force me will accomplish nothing.' But souls soon learn that a taste of something bitter can sometimes be preferable to sugar."

Addressing Mother Marie de Gonzague, she says: "I know very well that your little lambs think I am strict, but they can say what they like, for in their hearts they know that I really love them and that I shall never be like the hireling who runs away from his flock when he sees the wolf coming. I am ready to give my life for them, but my love for them is so disinterested that I don't want them to be aware of it. By God's grace, I have never tried to win their hearts. I know that my mission is to lead them to God and to make them know that here on earth you, Mother, take the place of Jesus and must be loved and respected."

Céline says that, in her first days as novice-mistress, Thérèse tried to resolve the novices' spiritual conflicts by reasoning with them and, if one novice complained of another, she would do her best to prove that the one thought to be in the wrong was really guiltless. This method started interminable discussions which led nowhere and were quite unprofitable spiritually. Thérèse very quickly realized this and at once changed her tactics.

Instead of trying to settle the troubles of the novices by endeavoring to show that there was no real reason behind them, she made them face up to them. Céline gives an example involving herself: "I might go to her and burst out with: 'Here it is, Saturday, and the novice who should have filled the firewood box hasn't done it, yet I never fail to do it when it's my turn!' " Thérèse made no attempt to deny that this was exasperating and even went as far as to say that the negligent novice very possibly had every fault Céline attributed to her. Then, after more or less agreeing with her sister, she would go on talking and, says Céline, "She gradually even got me to wish that the nuns would ignore me and never show me any consideration, that the novices would fail to do their allotted jobs and that I should be blamed for their neglect of their tasks, blamed too for having done badly something which I hadn't even been asked to do. Then, having brought me to this state, she would give me examples of hidden acts of virtue performed by the novice I had accused, so that soon all my resentment was swept away by admiration and I thought that every novice was better than I could ever be."

On this particular occasion, when the storm blew up over the firewood box, Thérèse had learned that the box had been filled between the time Céline saw it empty and the time she came to complain to her about it. Céline says: "She never mentioned this, although it would have ended my irritation at once. But when she had succeeded in bringing me round to a proper disposition she said very quietly: 'I know that the box is filled.' "

Thérèse has set down her principles for dealing with the novices: "They must not go to the trouble of approaching me if they are not prepared to be told the truth. Any reproof to a novice must be free from the least trace of passion. Kindness must not degenerate into weakness. When one is justified in finding fault, one must not worry at having given pain. It does one more harm than good to chase after the delinquent to try to console her. Left alone, she is forced to look beyond creatures and to turn to God; she is compelled to face up to her faults and to humble herself. Otherwise, she would expect to be comforted after every deserved rebuke, and would act like a spoiled child who stamps and screams until its mother returns and dries its tears."

Certainly Thérèse knew how to speak briskly to an erring novice. When one made her bed badly, Thérèse demanded: "Is that the way you would have made the bed of the Child Jesus?" One washday, a novice was sauntering towards the laundry, stopping every now and then to look at the flowers in the garden. Thérèse came up behind her and asked: "Is that the way people hurry to work who have children and have to earn the money to buy food for them?" A novice complained that she was much more tired than her companions because, in addition to her ordinary work, she had other tasks of which the others knew nothing. "Yes, of course," said Thérèse, "you feel this fatigue so much because no one is aware of it." Another novice, hoping to be congratulated on her virtue, told Thérèse of something she had done which she thought especially meritorious. Instead of the expected praise, she heard: "Compare this trifling deed with what Our Lord has the right to expect of you! You should humble yourself for having lost so many opportunities of showing your love for him."

She could tease as well as reprimand. A novice was much given to crying over trifles—as Thérèse had done years before. She was quite unable to control her tears until once, during a fit of weeping, Thérèse came up to her and tried to catch the tears in a mussel-shell. The novice was forced to laugh and Thérèse handed her the shell with permission to cry as much as she liked provided it was into the shell.

The novice often interrupted her at inopportune moments and pestered her with either silly or tactless questions, but her replies were never sharp or impatient. Her voice and face remained calm. She always greeted them with a smile and spoke gently, and this when, too ill to walk, she sat in an invalid chair in the garden. Both novices and nuns interrupted her continually. She showed no impatience, but put down her pen, closed her notebook and chatted with them. Asked by one of her sisters how she could endure this, she replied: "Well, as I am writing about brotherly love, I think it as well to practice it."

She would never allow her novices to brood about themselves, telling them that it was a sure way to sterilize the soul. When they began to feel themselves drifting towards a bout of introspection, they must, she told them, at once forget their own thoughts and feelings and hasten to perform some work of charity. Nor must they ever, unless it was essential, seek any modification of the Rule nor seek to be dispensed from any of the day-to-day work that had to be done. Nor, on the other hand, must they show too much zeal, for that could harm both themselves and others.

For example, during the annual retreat they were freed

from all manual work. Now they might be tempted to give a helping hand to some of the nuns. This would be a charitable act, but it would be better not to do it. The volunteer's fervor might die, yet she would feel an obligation to continue helping, though unwillingly, and the other novices, when they were in retreat, would imagine that they had to imitate her lest they should be thought lacking in charity. It was far better to stick to the Rule for "we are truly fortunate in having only to follow what our holy Mother Teresa has laid down for us."

The Carmelite Rule must be obeyed to its last letter. A few months after she entered Carmel, Céline complained to Thérèse that she found life there difficult. Thérèse pointed out that it was not really true for her to say that she could not do everything she wanted to: "I admit that you cannot follow your own will in all the round of daily life, but if you take life here as a whole, isn't that what you chose? So you are doing what you want by not doing it, for you knew very well what kind of a life you undertook when you came to Carmel. I assure you that I wouldn't stay here a moment under constraint. If people forced me to live like this, I could not endure it. But I want to live this life. I welcome all that goes against the grain. I welcome everything that thwarts my own will, for on the day of my profession, I openly declared that it was of my own free choice that I wanted to be a Carmelite nun. As we wish to be martyrs, we must use all the opportunities we have to make our life in religion a martyrdom."

To practice perfect obedience was one of these opportunities, and it was seized gladly by Thérèse herself and never kept for long from the attention of her novices. Céline came to her with yet another complaint. A nun had reproached her and she was quite sure she had not deserved any reprimand: "She was in the wrong and anyhow it was nothing to do with her." "That's true," Thérèse said, "but Our Lord did not say, 'Obey only your superiors,' but 'Give to every man who asks' and 'Whosoever will force thee one mile, go with him [an]other two.' "

One begins to feel sorry for Céline, aged twenty-five to Thérèse's twenty-one, a young woman who had stood aside to let Thérèse enter Carmel before her and who had stayed in the world, along with Léonie, to nurse their striken father, and who, at the age of eighteen, had been the closest confidante of fourteen-year old Thérèse. Yet, in Carmel, it is she who appears young and immature and who has to turn to Thérèse for instruction and consolation.

What is more, although Thérèse speaks to her with love—as she did to everyone—her voice has authority and an edge to it. Céline copied some of her poems on loose sheets of paper. A nun borrowed them and Céline was not too pleased. To Thérèse she said: "It would have been much more sensible to have copied them into a notebook. I might then have had some hope of getting them back." There was no comfort from her sister: "You should be glad to be deprived of them. Not only should you be delighted to lend them, but you should act in such a way that they'll be borrowed again. As you wrote your poems to help souls, it would be better to give them away rather than to lend them. Remember that St. Aloysius de Gonzague never asked for the return of anything he loaned."

Not easily rebuffed, Céline tackled her again, this time with a complaint that her work basket had been upset by someone and that one or two things were missing. Once again, Thérèse had to straighten her out: "You should be happy about this and tell yourself: 'I am so poor that it's quite natural for me to be without things and perfectly fitting for them to have been taken away from me as they weren't mine in the first place.' "

But this is the small change of conventual life, interesting because St. Thérèse is involved and because it reveals how quickly she had developed into a woman of remarkable clarity of mind and sureness of touch. When she was not dealing with a particular fault or problem, she of course gave wider spiritual direction, but there were never any hazy generalizations. Everything she said was as clear, precise and definite as this: "The most trivial act, one that no one knows about, provided it is inspired by love, is often of greater worth than the greatest achievement. It is not the value nor even the apparent holiness of deeds which counts, but only the love put into them. And no one can say that he cannot do these little things for God, for everyone is capable of them."

Much of what she told her novices has inevitably been lost, but it is evident that, even as she brought them closer to God, so did they her. The responsibility for the training of five souls is a heavy one. As we have seen, Thérèse admits she dared not . . . could not have shouldered it unaided, so she abandoned herself to God with the result, as she says, that her soul never made such progress.

Chapter 9

THE STORY OF A SOUL

Perhaps this is the place to remark on the speed with which Thérèse outgrew her sisters. As a child, first Pauline and then Marie looked after her, and what they said was almost the word of God. Once in Carmel, however, she rapidly overtook them. By this I do not mean that she in any way broke away from them, as a child, growing into womanhood, snaps many of the links that have bound her to her family. The love and veneration she had always felt for her elder sisters never diminished, but she could no longer accept them as her spiritual guides. When she was nineteen, Thérèse, writing to Céline, could say: "You know that Thérèse can achieve nothing without Céline. It needs both of them to do a complete job, and so it is for Céline to finish what Thérèse has begun."

Two years later, Thérèse was writing to Céline advising her on spiritual matters and asking her if she understood, and Céline was writing back to say how much good her sister's letters did her. And all her sisters felt the same. They were now the ones who sought instruction, who felt privileged to learn from her. Even as early as the time of Thérèse's profession, when she was nineteen, Marie wrote to her: "How quickly Jesus has made my little Thérèse develop!" And, prophetically: "Ah! Jesus alone knows what you are to Him. It's His secret which He will reveal to us one day."

When she was dying, they sat round her bed and sought to wring out of her every word she could utter about her relationship with God, knowing full well that there was between Him and her an understanding such as

123

is rarely granted to human beings. The sisters admitted that they wanted to get all the spiritual benefits they could from her last days on earth and so bombarded her with questions that Thérèse herself uttered the mild complaint: "I'm so harassed with questions that I feel like Joan of Arc before the tribunal."

One has sympathy with her sisters. They had believed for some years that, through Thérèse, they could themselves learn to know God better, that she was the channel through which many graces flowed, and that she was a saint—they used the word not as one of casual approbation for a good nun, but as the Church was to use it about her after her death. To them, long before she was canonized, she was not merely "our saintly little sister," but Saint Thérèse of the Child Jesus of the Holy Face. So it is easy to understand why they gave her so little peace on her deathbed.

Few people experience the certainty that they are talking with a saint; if they had that experience they would behave as Thérèse's sisters did. And how much we should have lost but for the persistence of Mother Agnés, sitting by the bed, questioning, uttering platitudes and the stale phrases of conventional piety, and writing down every word of her sister's replies. Again and again we have to stress the point that without the early training given her by her sisters, without their speedy recognition of her greatness and without their prescience of what she was to become with her death, it is unlikely that any of us would have heard of Thérèse Martin.

One nun in the Carmel said: "I cannot help wondering what our Mother Prioress will find to say about Sister Thérèse when she dies. It will be very difficult, for though the little Sister is very good she has never done anything worth speaking about." One of her novices was more enlightened. She suddenly knelt one day before Thérèse, clasped her hands together, bowed her head and exclaimed: "Oh, Sister Thérèse of the Child Jesus, you are not like the others. I'm sure that after your death we shall kneel and say: 'St. Thérèse of the Child Jesus, pray for us." She was right, but if it were not for her sisters and Mother Marie de Gonzague, we should have to agree with the nun who saw nothing extraordinary in Thérèse.

When Thérèse was dead, her body was buried in the Lisieux cemetery, and that could have been the end of her as far as future generations were concerned, just as it is for most nuns and, indeed, for almost all of us. She left behind a manuscript written in three cheap notebooks, some verses and some letters. Other nuns have done the same and the pages of their writings yellow with age in the archives of their convents. Yet not a single day now passes without scores of people buying the autobiography of St. Thérèse, which now can be read in forty languages. That this is so is due to three of her sisters, Marie, Pauline and Céline, and also Mother Marie de Gonzague.

I must not be misunderstood. Let me quote St. Thomas of Aquinas: "God's planning and arranging immediately engage every event, though His Providence is carried out executively and the world is governed through secondary cause." In other words, God uses people for His purposes. Now in the Carmel of Lisieux, apart from the novice I have mentioned above, only these four women saw in Thérèse a being who lived on a wholly different level from the other nuns, including themselves. Only her sisters, who had known her all her life, were able to see what burned behind the quiet, smiling presence of the young nun who seemed neither to do nor say anything extraordinary.

Mother Marie de Gonzague, perhaps supernaturally enlightened, noted the mettle of Thérèse when she was still a postulant. Such enlightenment may have been given her because, at key periods during Thérèse's life and after her death, she had the power to exercise a veto which could have ensured that nothing of Thérèse's writings ever saw the light. Had she wished, she would have been perfectly within her rights to have put them into the fire. Judging by some of her outbursts of temperament, it would not have been surprising had she done this. But no. She was one of the most indefatigable workers in the task of seeing that Thérèse became known outside the cloisters of Carmel.

It was, as we have seen, Marie, the eldest sister of Thérèse, who set in motion the writing of the autobiography; it was Mother Agnès who gave the order for it to be written; and it was Mother Marie de Gonzague who allowed it to be published. At the time that she wrote them, Thérèse had no idea that the pages she produced for Mother Agnès and for Marie would be published. Those she wrote on the order of Mother Marie de Gonzague were started in June and finished at the very beginning of July, 1897—three months before she died—and Céline has said that Thérèse thought this portion would not be published as it was written, but that it would be made use of in a volume published to reveal the path by which she had gone to God and so encourage others to tread the same path.

Later, as she drew nearer death, she began to see the importance of all she had written and to insist that it must be published. What she wrote for Mother Marie de Gonzague was the result of Mother Agnès determination. For some time Mother Marie was not aware that Thérèse had written anything, for she had been replaced as prioress by Mother Agnès. At the end of the three-year term of office of Mother Agnès, she was, however, re-elected prioress, which meant that any further writing by Thérèse must have her consent.

Mother Agnès has told what happened: "I was afraid that Mother Marie de Gonzague would not think these writings as interesting as I did, so I dared not speak to her about them. But, as Thérèse was so ill, I finally decided to broach the matter." It was midnight on June 2, 1897, when she went to see Mother Marie—not, one would think, the most suitable time to be chosen by anyone so nervous as Mother Agnès says she was. She told her prioress that she could not go to sleep without telling her a secret: "When I was prioress, Sister Thérèse jotted down some memories of her childhood. She did this to please me—by obedience. They are delightful, but they won't give you much help when you come to write her obituary, for they say very little about her life in Carmel. But she could produce something much more useful if you ordered her to."

It was another victory for Mother Agnès, the master tactician. Next day, Mother Marie ordered Thérèse to continue the story of her life.

Four months later, Thérèse was dead and the sisters swung into action. The prioress gave her consent for the manuscripts to be published—on one condition: that it was made to appear that all three manuscripts had been addressed to her. Shortly afterwards, when a copy had been made of the manuscripts, she decided to burn them so as to destroy the evidence of her duplicity, but Mother Agnès offered to alter on the original pages all references which showed that most of them had not been written for her. So they were saved.

The manuscript text was sent to Father Godefroid Madelaine, the prior of an abbey in the neighborhood. He was a good friend of Carmel and had known Thérèse. He was asked to examine it and give his views on whether it should be published. We do not know if he saw the original text or the one edited by Mother Agnès. He studied it for three months and his verdict was that it contained details that were so intimate and that some parts of it were so far above the usual run of spiritual writings that it would be better to omit these.

He thought, too, there were some slight faults of grammar and of style and some repetition. But it was with "immense pleasure and spiritual satisfaction" that he had read "these pages impregnated with divine love." He told Mother Marie he would mark with a blue pencil the passages he thought should be cut, but, long afterwards, at the canonization process he said that he had made only very trifling corrections. The most he did was to split up the text into chapters and suggest the title *The Story of a Soul* instead of *A Canticle of Love, Or The Passing of an An-*

gel, which the Carmel had put forward. On March 7, 1898, Father Godefroid took the manuscript to the Bishop of Bayeux, who gave it his *Imprimatur* but refused to write an introduction.

On September 30, 1898, a year to the day after the death of Thérèse, *The Story of a Soul* was published in an edition of two thousand copies. There was great nervousness in the Carmel at the size of this edition. Copies went to other Carmels in place of the obituary which is usually sent after the death of a nun, but these accounted for only a small number, and it was feared that most of the volumes would be left on Carmel's hands. How absurd these fears seem in the light of what we know now! This life story of a good little nun in a small French town published by a provincial firm, a story which contained nothing apparently out of the ordinary and which was written in a style differing little from that disfiguring so many books of piety—this is the story which has become one of the great best sellers of our time.

In twelve years it sold forty-seven thousand copies; between 1910 and 1915 another hundred and sixty-four thousand were sold; by 1932 the total was well over three million copies in France alone. Today the figure has risen to many millions and in nearly every language. Not every reader of the first edition was enthusiastic. Three Carmels disliked it and there was criticism of its "great sentimentality." Very much later, in 1921, a Vatican decree which proclaimed that Thérèse had lived a life of heroic virtue mentioned her autobiography and declared that, attractive and fascinating though it was, the salutary results produced by reading it could not possibly be explained except by "the action of divine grace." Father Pichon, the Jesuit who had been so intimate with the Martin family, came to the same conclusion, declaring that the incredible manner in which her reputation spread was "entirely inexplicable" without an extraordinary intervention of Providence, and that no advertising campaign could account for the fascination exerted by *The Story of a Soul*.

There is no doubt that the book generated its own publicity. Carmelites and a few high dignitaries of the Church read it first; then lent it to their friends who then wanted their own copies, which in turn were lent to their friends. Letters began to arrive at the Lisieux Carmel demanding more copies, along with pictures and relics of Thérèse. Twelve years after her death, there were fifty letters a day. Thousands upon thousands of pictures were turned out with a fragment of stuff used or touched by Thérèse attached to them. The organization of this was the work of Céline. From her sister's death to her canonization—a period of twenty-eight years—more than thirty million pictures and over seventeen million relics were distributed. Ill-informed and possibly malicious voices have said that St. Thérèse was manufactured by her sisters. In their hands, her cult became an industry and the Carmel a propaganda factory. The sisters were certainly industrious, but they did not create the demand for the pictures and relics. They satisfied it, and it was a demand which snowballed day by day.

The two thousand copies of *The Story of a Soul* were the catalyst which started the immense chain reaction, still continuing unabated in its intensity. After they were published, the sisters were but tools to serve the all-conquering cult. To use the language of the market place, no amount of publicity will keep a bad product selling and selling and selling. No efforts by the sisters nor indeed by the whole Carmelite Order could have induced millions to buy and to read the book; even less would it have been possible for them to persuade the Church to canonize its author had she been unworthy. We may, perhaps without irreverence, say that once the book had appeared God intervened directly, but that to ensure its appearance He used Mother Agnès as His agent and she persuaded Mother Marie de Gonzague to agree with and support her designs.

It must here be said that many of those who read St. Thérèse's autobiography in any edition published before 1956 had to overcome a strong revulsion against its phrasing. There was a sickliness about it, a cloying sweetness that was often hard to stomach. It says much for the power and vitality of her message that it succeeded in burning through the stale, sugary words in which it was wrapped. The wrapping was done by Mother Agnès.

As I have said, Thérèse, when she was near death, suddenly realized the importance of her book and urged Mother Agnès to get it published at all cost. She said to her sister: "You must take out or add anything you want to this story of my life. It will be just as though I did it. Remember this later and have no scruples." Mother Agnès took full advantage of this. She rewrote Thérèse's autobiography. These words were not mine. They were those of the Carmelite priest and scholar who was entrusted, at the death of Mother Agnès, with the task of producing a facsimile edition of the manuscripts as they were written by Thérèse.

Mother Agnès, we recall, taught Thérèse for several years, and to the autobiography she brought the same mind that had carefully corrected the grammar, the punctuation and the phrasing of her sister's childish essays. In doing so, she effectively destroyed its whole tone and flavor. She left its matter intact, except for many anecdotes which it was reasonable to omit as they were about people who were still alive when the book came out.

Let us look at some of the changes made by Mother Agnès—there are about seven thousand of them altogether. Thérèse said: "Oh! God is so good to me that I cannot possibly be afraid of Him." Pauline's version is: "Oh! How happy God makes me! How easy and pleasant it is to serve Him!" Thérèse compares the spiritual world to God's garden. The great saints are the roses and lilies, but the humbler flowers are also created by God and are equally pleasing to Him. Pauline adds: "The more joyfully the flowers do His will, the greater is their perfection." This replaces Thérèse's: "Perfection consists in doing His will, in being what He wants us to be." Thérèse said: "I never forget what I am." Pauline translates it into: "I never forget what a miserable creature I am."

And a "happy memory" becomes a "particularly fragrant memory." A "grace" is transformed into an "unutterable grace."

Many pages could be filled with similar examples of the heavy hand of Mother Agnès at work, examples which show that she had no understanding of a natural, unaffected style. To words she was tone-deaf. It must be noted that the Church, before she beatified and later canonized Thérèse, had examined all she wrote as it was when she put down her pen. The Church was not fobbed off with an amended version.

While we are considering the part played by Mother Agnès in making her sister's sanctity known, it is worth considering the fact that Thérèse died at the age of twenty-four; that Léonie, the sister who was a Visitation nun, lived to seventy-eight; and that the ages of the three Carmelite sisters at their death were as follows: Marie, a month short of eighty; Pauline, eighty-nine; and Céline, also eighty-nine. Is it fanciful to see the will of God in this, particularly in the case of Pauline and Céline, the two sisters who did, humanly speaking, far more than anyone else to spread Thérèse's message? But all four of them gave evidence about their sister before the two tribunals set up to examine testimony affecting the possibility of her being raised to the altar. They alone could speak with authority about her as a child and a young girl. Without their evidence, the dossier on Thérèse assembled by the ecclesiastical authorities would have been sadly incomplete.

Thérèse herself had no need to reach old age. Years before she died, she said: "It seems to me that love can take the place of a long life. Jesus takes no notice of time, as there is none in Heaven. He takes account only of love." A few weeks before she died she thought the same: "One's age means nothing to God." But it was necessary that the closest witnesses of her life and virtues should survive long after she had gone. And so they did.

It is to Mother Agnès that we owe most. Without her

energy, will, and powers of organization, the likelihood is that Thérèse would be not even a footnote in the history of her Carmel. Thérèse knew what her "little mother" had been to her: "I cannot express how grateful I am. I have to cry when I think of all you have done for me since I was a small child. Oh! How much I owe to you! But when I'm in heaven I shall reveal the truth. I shall say to the saints: 'It is my little mother who is responsible for all that you find pleasing to me.' "

When she was in her late eighties, Mother Agnès told a pleasing story: "Last night I had a dream in which I saw Thérèse looking just the same as when she was alive. She smiled at me and said: 'You are growing old, my little mother.' I told her: 'You couldn't have said anything that pleases me more.' "

As a girl of sixteen, when Thérèse was four, Pauline wrote: "I love having my Thérèse with me, for then I feel that no harm can touch me." It is fitting that the last words of Mother Agnès, uttered a moment before she died, were: "Little St. Thérèse, help me. Come to fetch me."

Chapter 10

"SPIRITUAL CHILDHOOD"— A PROPHECY

"When I think of you, my darling Father, I naturally think of God," Thérèse wrote in a letter to Mr. Martin from Carmel. These were no words of mere endearment. As always, Thérèse meant exactly what she said. It is this feeling for her father and all that she felt for her father at home, both at Alençon and Lisieux, which colored her whole attitude to God. By saying "colored" I do not imply any distortion; her attitude is the right one, the only one, for it is that taught us by Our Lord. One might think the approach of Thérèse to God, her feeling toward Him, and her thoughts about Him are those of all Christians. Unhappily, they are not. Nor were they during Thérèse's life nor for many centuries before. Some Christians have felt as she did, but many more have not. God as Judge has too often replaced God as father. God is a judge, the Supreme Judge, but as St. Thomas Aquinas says: "God is merciful. He works above His justice, not against it," and also, in words that would have delighted Thérèse: "The more we love God, the less we fear punishment."

As a child and a young girl, Thérèse had never feared punishment. Why should she? Her parents loved her and she loved them, and the same currents of love flowed between her and her sisters. Those set in authority above her were never ill-tempered or arbitrary in their orders, nor did they ever seek to make her obey rules that were harsh or unfair. So, loving them as she did, obedience was easy for her. If she did transgress, she was sorry and ran to be forgiven. This forgiveness was given instantly, and her misdemeanor was as if it had never been.

133

Her good behavior as a child naturally owed something to her temperament. She says: "Even before I was three, there was no need to scold me. A single, gentle word was sufficient then and has always been enough to make me see and repent my wrongdoings," and her sister, Marie, says the same: "She never had to be scolded. If we said: 'That is wrong' or 'That displeases God,' she would never offend in that way again."

She was not, though, a docile child, but a very lively and spirited one, yet any natural impulses to naughtiness were overwhelmed by love. Throughout her life she loved passionately "Oh! The happy carelessness, the blissful intoxication of love! Love which gives everything without thought! Too often, though, we give only after careful thought and hesitate to sacrifice our worldly and spiritual interests. That's not love. Love is blind, a torrent which sweeps everything away." She is one of history's great lovers in the best and highest sense of the word.

When she was eighteen, she could think of heaven as a re-creation of the happy life she had spent at home. "Céline darling," she says, "the fashion of the world passes, the shadows withdraw, and soon we shall be in our native land, soon the joys of our childhood, those Sunday evenings and our intimate talks will all be restored to us—forever, and with interest. Then we shall see waves of light pouring from the dazzling head of our beloved father and each of his white hairs will shine like a sun and pour joy and happiness upon us."

At twenty she could still write about Heaven in the same terms—this time to Léonie: "There we shall all be together again, never to part. For all eternity we shall enjoy the bliss of family life; we shall see again our dearest father surrounded with honor and glory for his perfect fidelity and especially for the humiliations of which he has had to drink so deeply; we shall see our good mother, who will rejoice at the trials which were our lot during our earthly exile, and we shall take great delight at her happiness as she gazes at her five daughters—all of them nuns. Together with the four little angels who are awaiting us up there, we shall form a crown which will encircle for ever the brows of our beloved parents."

Heaven was for her but a glorified Les Buissonnets where time stood still and the tranquil pleasures of her youth would be renewed and never end. But long before she died, this naive, childlike conception of Heaven had gone, replaced by one which cannot be described in cozy, comfortable terms in letters to her sisters. Speaking of this Heaven, she says: "I have one expectation which makes my heart beat faster: the love which I shall receive and then be able to give." And a year before she died, she writes of God as the divine Eagle and of herself as a little bird, and sees death and Heaven in these terms: "I hope that one day, my adored Eagle, You will swoop down to your little bird, mount with her to the source of love and plunge her into the fiery abyss of that love to which she has offered herself as a victim."

A far cry from the quiet, lamplit winter evenings at Les Buissonnets. But it was the days of her childhood which set her feet on the path leading to these heights of spiritual passion. All her life she had known love. It was never possible for her to doubt for one single moment that her father loved her. He was always present and to her child's mind was all-powerful, all-wise and all-good. His kindness to her was never exhausted. His benevolence was without bounds. He was her "king," she his "little queen." Never could she have imagined being alienated from him; whatever wrong she might do, she knew, with the same certainty that she knew she was alive, that one word of contrition would have brought instant and complete reconciliation.

As she grew older and thought, not more often but more profoundly, about God, she behaved to Him as she did to her earthly father, giving Him perfect love and trust, so she never knew any fear of God. His majesty, His power, the fact that one cannot fall into hyperbole in speaking of Him—so infinitely does He exceed all our imaginings—all this was known to Thérèse, but the difference between the Creator and His creatures neither worried nor frightened her.

One of her favorite sayings of Our Lord was "For whosoever shall do the will of my Father, that is in heaven, he is my brother, and sister, and mother." She realized fully that Our Lord is the King of Glory, throned high above the cherubims and that the heavens cannot contain His splendor. Yet how foolish He was—yes, that is the word she uses—to descend to earth to make friends of sinners, to make them His intimates and "like unto Himself." And she told a novice who was fretting over her faults: "You mustn't be afraid, for He you have chosen for your Spouse has every imaginable perfection—but He is blind and so ignorant of arithmetic that He cannot even add up. Were He clear-sighted enough to see all our sins, if He were good enough at figures to be able to tot up their number, He would send us straight back to our nothingness. But His love for us makes Him blind. But to make Him blind and unable to count the number of our sins, we must approach Him through His Heart—on that side He is defenseless." To her sister Léonie she wrote: "I assure you that God is much kinder than you think. A glance, a sigh of love satisfies Him. I myself find it very easy to practice perfection, for I know that all one has to do is to take Jesus by His Heart." She has complete confidence: "Even if I had on my conscience every sin it is possible to commit, I should fling myself, my heart broken with sorrow, into the arms of Jesus, for I know how He loves the prodigal child who returns to Him."

She continually stresses the supreme importance of this confidence: "It is trust and trust alone that must guide us to Love . . . fear will lead us to that strict justice which is shown to sinners, but it is not that justice which Jesus will show to those who love Him." She urges us all to live "the life of trust and love." It is this insistence on an absolute confidence which is at the heart of her "little way of spiritual childhood." God is our Father; we are His children. Therefore, we love and trust Him and we know that He needs nothing from us and that all we can offer Him has been first bestowed upon us by Him. We must realize that all our works count for nothing in themselves. This is not to say that good works are not to be done. We must perform them continually, but do them because we love God, not because we think they have an intrinsic value. God cares nothing for the deed itself, but He cares greatly about the most trivial act if it is done to please Him and to show that we love Him. We can never deserve His love but, as Thérèse says, "We must say to Him: 'I know I can never be worthy of all the things I hope for, but I hold my hand out to You like a poor beggar and I know You will give me more than I want because You are so good.'"

She has described what she means by remaining like a little child before God: "One has to recognize one's nothingness and to expect to get everything from God, just as a child looks to its father for everything. One must not take credit for one's virtues, nor believe oneself capable of anything, but must realize that it is God who places virtues in the hand of His little child for use when he needs them. But these virtues never cease to be God's. Finally, one must never be discouraged by his failings, for children are always falling down, but they are too small to do themselves much harm." Further, she declares: "The moment He sees that we realize our nothingness, He stretches out His hand to us." Touchingly, she confesses that for years she has often dropped off to sleep during the hours devoted to contemplative prayers and during her thanksgiving after Holy Communion: "I ought to be very upset but I'm not, for I know that children are loved just as much by their parents when they are asleep as when they are awake."

How, I imagine, St. Thérèse would have relished the story of one of the great and saintly Fathers of the Desert. Some monks asked him: "Father, when we see some of our brethren asleep during prayers, shouldn't we go and shake them awake?" His answer was: "If I were to see a brother overcome by sleep, I should want to lay his head

on my knees so that he could rest comfortably." In another reference to her falling asleep, she says that the moment she wakes, she resumes loving God. She knows that
she does not get enough sleep in Carmel and that, although she wants to stay awake, she cannot help dropping
off, but as she says: "The Lord has a father's pity: does
He not know the stuff of which we are made; can He
forget that we are only dust?"

Shortly before her death, she was talking to her sisters
about God and instead of saying "Father," she used the
word "Papa." Her sisters laughed, but she at once took
them up and declared: "Why yes, He really is my Papa
and I love to call Him that," and how breathtaking is the
confidence with which she says: "I talk very simply to
God, saying what I want to say, and He always under-
stands me." And, ravaged by tuberculosis, hardly able to
eat, and gasping for breath, she gave in one short sentence what she meant when she spoke of holiness:
"Holiness does not consist of any one particular method
of spirituality: it is a disposition of the heart which makes
us small and humble within the arms of God, aware of
our weakness but almost rashly confident in His fatherly
goodness."

During the last weeks of her life, Thérèse uttered some
remarkable words. At a first reading, they are shattering.
Earlier in her life we have heard her saying that she
wanted to be as insignificant as a grain of sand, and the
slightest acquaintance with her writings and her life must
show that her humility was true and deep. Time and time
again, from her early adolescence, she repeated and made
her own the words of St. John of the Cross: "Oh Lord, to
suffer and be despised for You!"

Yet in those hot, pain-racked days of August and September more than seventy years ago, she spoke of her future with an assurance which, in anyone else, would be
dismissed as arrogant posturing. Let us imagine the scene.
She is in the small, bare infirmary, lying on her bed,
propped up on pillows. Her flesh is wasted by disease,

sweat pours down her face, great spasms of coughing shake her, and her soul is plunged into darkness. Mother Agnès of Jesus, Marie, and Céline never leave her in peace. Mother Agnès sits by her bed with a pencil and notebook. Céline also has a notebook. "It was hard on Thérèse," Mother Agnès admits, "but she let me do it so as not to sadden me." Sometimes, Thérèse and Céline used the private language of their childhood, which was incomprehensible to the other nuns, but mostly the exchange between the sisters was a matter of straight-forward questions and answers.

Her sisters were sure that they sat around the bedside of a saint, and before she left them for heaven, they were determined to draw from her every word that would confirm this conviction. Some of their questions were silly; others moving. Many of Thérèse's replies either amplify or stress points she had already made in her autobiography and in her letters, but there are others.

It was in March, 1897, that she gave the first hint of the nature of these replies. She was not bedridden then, but in a note to Mother Agnès she said: "Oh yes, Jesus loves you and so do I. Every day He gives you proof of it, but I don't. But when I'm in heaven, my little arm will stretch a long way and you will hear news of it."

In the infirmary one night, she said to her sisters: "You know, don't you, that you are looking after a little saint."

She declared that, after her death, she would let fall a shower of roses. She had a habit of scattering rose petals over her crucifix as a gesture of love to Our Lord. On her deathbed, she asked for them to be gathered up and looked after carefully: "One day they will give happiness to many souls."

When she was asked if she would look down from Heaven, her answer was: "No, I shall come down!" Another remark was: "In this world all passes away, even little Thérèse. But she will return!" After looking at a picture of St. Joan of Arc in prison, she said: "The saints encourage me, too, in my prison. They tell me: 'As long as you are in chains, you cannot fulfill your mission, but later, after your death, will come the time of your conquests.' "

She wrote: "I am quite sure I shall not be idle in heaven. I want to keep on working for the Church and for souls. I keep asking God to allow me to do this and I am certain that He will. The angels always see the Face of God and are plunged in the boundless ocean of His love, and yet they are continually looking after us. Why should Jesus not allow me to do the same?" And again: "I shall give God no peace until He has given me all that I want ... Jesus has always made me desire what He wished to give me. So, in Heaven, is He going to begin not to grant my wishes? I certainly cannot believe that, so I say to you: 'Soon, little Brother, I shall be with you.' " Here she was writing to a future missionary priest, and to him she also wrote: "I can't foresee the future, but if Jesus fulfills my hopes about it, I promise to continue to be your little sister when I'm in Heaven. Far from being broken, our union will become closer, for then there will no longer be any enclosure or any grills, and my soul will be free to fly with you to the most distant missions."

Céline mentioned to her sister that the nuns in the Carmel of Saigon probably still thought she would be going out to them, and Thérèse, almost casually, said: "I shall be with them very soon. Once I am in Heaven, I shall make my rounds very swiftly."

Of her autobiography she said to Mother Agnès: "These pages will do much good," and then added: "Ah! How well I know that everyone will love me." Marie remarked to her one day that she was afraid she would never be able to comfort Mother Agnès in the grief she would feel at her death. "Oh! You mustn't worry about that!" Thérèse exclaimed. "Mother Agnès won't have time to feel distressed, for until she dies, she'll be kept so busy with me that she'll scarcely suffer at all."

Pope Benedict XV referred to these statements, saying: "Seeing that throughout her life she gave constant proof of her humility, she could not pronounce words apparently contrary to that virtue, unless under the empire, or beneath the direct inspiration of a Divine command." These words, as those of a Pope, must be treated with the greatest respect, and it is true that Thérèse, who wished to be regarded as "a little grain of sand" would not have uttered these vainglorious prophecies about herself unless, by doing so, she had not been serving God's purpose. But God does not overrule His creatures. He does not, that is, impose upon us modes of behavior or expression which are contrary to our real feelings.

It must be realized that Thérèse had a very literal mind. She had been told and she knew that God was her Father; she knew that her natural father would deny her nothing, so why should her heavenly Father? It was, to her, as simple as that. She was well aware that she had denied God nothing and, with unshaken confidence, she felt that He, in return, would give her all that she desired. Would she have felt this with the same certainty had she not known the unbounded love of her father? During her childhood, Mr. Martin was the image of God to her and though, as she grew older, she learned that her father was but a simulacrum of her Creator, it would be psychologically impossible for her to root out from her mind a conception of God based on the knowledge of her father. There was no reason why she should: God Himself chose the title of father as the one best fitted to describe his relationship to us. And to Thérèse, with her father continually in mind, there could be no fitter title, none better able to describe her link with God.

Chapter 11

THE PROVIDENCE OF PICTURES

During most of history, men have been taught by words—spoken, written or printed—and for many centuries the human race has been remarkably indifferent to the appearance of things and of people. The great rulers of the world had themselves reproduced in stone, but this was basically to satisfy the needs of statecraft. Statues of the Roman emperors appeared in forums throughout their realm, not to satisfy the curiosity of the ruled about their rulers, but to make disparate races aware that they formed a unity by virtue of their common allegiance to Caesar. If we consider the writers of the ancient world, we notice that there are few descriptions—and those are scanty—of the physical appearance of people. In his lives of the emperors, Suetonius gives a line or two regarding the looks of his protagonists, but he is an exception. We know nothing, for example, of the appearance of the Apostles. It is obvious, I think, that no one was interested in what the people he read about looked like.

But with the Renaissance, man took a new pride in himself, a pride that embraced his body, his clothes, his jewels; and so, nearly everyone of position and wealth was drawn or painted. Such portraits were too expensive for most people, and it was not until the invention of photography that the faces of the poor and humble were given immortality. Now we have moving pictures on the cinema and television screens, and the printed word is losing some of its power. More and more we too demand a picture to be convinced.

Had Thérèse lived in the eighteenth century, we should have no portrait of her; had Thérèse, living in the nineteenth century, not had a sister who was an enthusiastic photographer, we should not know her face; had the Carmel of Lisieux not been—for a Carmel—a strangely free-and-easy community, we might have had a photograph of her taken as she was lying in the chapel after her death and that is all. One may ask: but is it important that we be able to see her face? Does it matter?

St. Thérèse has suffered from two handicaps, one of which has already been discussed: the revision of the original manuscript of her autobiography by Mother Agnès of Jesus, a revision which removed all the sparkle of her style and greatly muted the vigor of her personality. Then we have the picture of her which for many years after her death, was issued by Carmel. Rarely can a saint have suffered so much at the hands of those devoted to her. This picture, put out as the official one—with approval—was described by the Bishop of Bayeux and Lisieux in 1915 as "a very conscientious and most carefully studied synthesis of the best features" of all the photographs of her possessed by Carmel.

The Bishop was a well-meaning man and an honest one. But he overlooked the one fault possessed by the official portrait: it bears no resemblance to St. Thérèse. The issue of this portrait must, of course, have been authorized by Mother Agnès, but it was Céline who produced it. Now it would have been a brave nun, foolhardy even, who would have ventured to speak ill of this picture to Céline. Céline called herself a female Boanerges—"a daughter of thunder"—and the thunder would have rolled around the head of any hostile critic.

Today, however, we can utter our criticism safely; by now, Céline knows she was mistaken, knows too that the controlled power which burns in the real face of her sister is something which should never have been destroyed by her attempts to prettify it. Céline in this life, however, was convinced that a photograph could not reveal the personality of the sitter. One has to admit that it was then impossible to take an instant, revealing shot. Not long before she died, Thérèse had to remain posed, motionless, for three periods of nine seconds before Céline could produce a satisfactory photograph. But Céline was wrong in thinking that this enforced immobility of the subject destroyed any chance of character emerging from the plate. We have only to look at Nadar's magnificent portrait of Baudelaire and at the work of Octavius Hill and Lewis Carrol to see what brutally or charmingly revealing pictures could come from the clumsy cameras of the last century.

But neither Céline nor the other nuns at Carmel were satisfied with what she produced, and so she painted her version of Thérèse, and that became the authentic portrait. The nuns were delighted. A former novice of Thérèse exclaimed: "It's just as if I'm seeing her again." One would not expect the nuns to disapprove of a portrait approved by their prioress, the saint's sister, and one which had been painted by another sister. Mr. and Mrs. Guérin, exercising the freedom given them by their status as uncle and aunt of the saint, made it very plain that they were far from pleased by it, and their daughter, Jeanne, and her husband, Dr. La Néele, would have nothing to do with Céline's production. They had copies made of two photographs of Thérèse as a novice, taken by a priest, which they distributed as a counterblast to Céline's work.

But reproductions of the official picture poured out—more than eight million copies of it were printed in France alone before 1915—and, grotesque though it is when set alongside the real portraits, we can say, in the words of an eminent Carmelite priest: "Yet Thérèse has used this picture to make herself known throughout the world. By it she has entered huts in the bush, the tents of nomads and the igloos of the North and spread her influence among them." But it has been reported that when one of the photographs of her was shown to a student who had hitherto seen only the official portrait he exclaimed: "It is almost like the face of a female Christ."

That remark explains the importance of being presented with the true likeness of St. Thérèse. We have now, as I have said, acquired the habit of demanding to see events and people as they happen and as they are. An insatiable visual curiosity has to be satisfied. Fundamentally, it is not in the least important what Thérèse looked like, but it is important that, if we are to be offered a likeness, it should be a true one. Truth always matters. Nor would it be important to see her face if it were not what it is. To believe that *every* face mirrors the person is mere superstition. Regard Himmler and consider his deeds. Read *The Decline and Fall of the Roman Empire* and between each chapter glance at a portrait of Gibbon and wonder that such genius could hide behind so prim and pursy a mask.

But the face of St. Thérèse needs no painted halo to tell us that we are looking at a saint. We can say more: we are gazing at sanctity itself. There is a photograph of her when she was eight years of age. She looks a very nice, strong-willed little girl. We have one of her at fifteen, that which shows her for the first time with her hair done up in grown-up style. The will is there; so is intelligence, and goodness illuminates the face. They are pleasant portraits for a family album. Then we come to those taken within the walls of Carmel. Nearly all are remarkable; three are outstanding. One of them was taken in March, 1896, another in July of the same year, and the third in June, 1897, three months before her death. In all of them she is looking straight at the camera lens. One shows her with a slight smile on her lips and in her eyes; in another, there is no smile, and it has an intensity that has yet no strain about it; and in the third, the one so near her death, we have the saint. Her face shows no trace of her illness. It is serene and yet quite unforgettable, so fully alive is it with the life that only perfect union with God can give.

St. Augustine writes of the growth of the love of God: "It begins, progresses, grows great and becomes perfect," and it would be easy to select photographs of St. Thérèse showing this growth mirrored in her face, although in this last photograph we have a face that has ceased to be a mirror; it is interpenetrated with divinity and, gazing at it, we think of those words of her sister, Marie: "You are possessed by God, literally *possessed*." Perhaps, after all, Céline and the Carmel were wiser than we know in hiding the real face of the saint for so long, for the reality is profoundly disturbing: "Cover her face; mine eyes dazzle." The official portrait is innocuous. It could not startle anyone, only soothe, but to meet the gaze of holiness is a very different matter. So, possibly Céline's brush and the blue pencil of Mother Agnès may have served the purpose of introducing their sister gently to the world. One does not and cannot know. We know only that Thérèse has broken through all the limitations imposed on her.

We must be eternally grateful to Céline and to Mother Marie de Gonzague and to Mother Agnès for this gallery of pictures of St. Thérèse, to the two prioresses for allowing Céline to use her camera, and to Céline for the skill and enthusiasm she brought to the task. All convents then regarded photography as a frivolous pastime, certainly not one to be countenanced within the enclosure; yet the Lisieux Carmel, with an astonishing indifference to the spirit of Carmelite asceticism, encouraged a postulant to enter with her camera and gave her every opportunity to use it. Forty-one negatives of St. Thérèse exist, showing her alone or in a group. They provide a unique pictorial documentation of the physical envelope of a saint. It is not easy to believe that this treasure fell into our hands by chance.

Chapter 12

A MISSIONARY FOR THE CHURCH

Mrs. Martin longed for sons. She was given two, but each of them lived for less than a year, and so she was denied the fulfillment of a great ambition: to give two missionary priests to the Church. On the death of the second, her sister wrote from her convent in Le Mans a prescient letter of consolation: "Your unshakable faith and confidence will one day be magnificently rewarded. Won't you have a rich recompense if God decides to give you that great saint you've longed so much to have for His glory?"

Mrs. Martin died before Thérèse was old enough to hear from her lips of her desire for sons who would be missionary priests, but she must have been told of it scores of times by her sisters, and in the impassioned outburst to Our Lord contained in that part of her autobiography written in response to Marie's appeal, she says: "I would like to travel throughout the world, preach Your Name and set Your glorious Cross on heathen soil but, my Beloved, one mission wouldn't be enough for me. I should want to preach the Gospel in all five continents and on the most remote islands, nor would I want to be a missionary for only a few years. I'd like to have been one from the creation of the world and to go on being one until its end."

In this outburst of love she also cries that she feels she could be a warrior for the Church, a priest, an apostle, a Doctor of the Church, and a martyr. But she had always felt the pull of the missions. During her visit to Rome, one of her fellow pilgrims gave her a copy of a magazine devoted to the labors of missionaries. She would not read

147

it. She gave her reason to Marie: "I have too keen a longing to offer myself to such work, and yet my real desire is to hide myself in the cloister so that I can give myself more fully to God." Towards the end of her life, there was the possibility that one or two of the nuns in the Carmel of Lisieux would be sent to a Carmel in Indo-China, and she said: "Since I entered the ark of Carmel, I've always thought that if Jesus didn't carry me off to Heaven very quickly, my lot would be that of Noe's little dove: God would one day open the window of the ark and tell me to fly far, far away to heathen shores, carrying with me a tiny olive branch. The thought of this made my soul soar high above all created things."

She goes on to explain that to leave her own Carmel would be painful, that she did not expect she would be of much use in a Carmel in a foreign country, and that she would then know real suffering, what she calls "the exile of the heart." And yet Mother Marie de Gonzague had told her that a special vocation was needed to live in a Carmel in the mission field and that she, Thérèse, had it. That, no doubt, was why she gave her the task of praying for and corresponding with two missionaries, Father Roulland and the Abbé Bellière.

Father Roulland had asked the prioress of the Lisieux Carmel to pick one of her nuns who would associate herself with his missionary work in China. Mother Marie de Gonzague gave him Thérèse, saying: "Of my good ones, she is the best—the dear little creature is wholly God's." In her first letter to him, Thérèse wrote: "I shall be very happy to work with you for the salvation of souls. That was the reason I became a Carmelite, but as I could not be an active one, I wanted to be one through love and penance, like our Mother, St. Theresa."

Thirty years after her death, a Vatican decree announced that Pope Pius XI had "been pleased to declare St. Thérèse of the Child Jesus 'Principal Patroness of all Missionaries,' whether men or women, and of all missions existing throughout the world, the equal of St. Francis

Xavier." Thus did God answer Mrs. Martin's prayers that she should give a missionary to the Church.

To have missionary sons was one of the great ambitions of Mr. and Mrs. Martin, but though missionaries had a great appeal for them, they basically wanted sons who would become priests, missionaries if possible, but that would have been, as it were, a luxury. To have a son a priest, whether at home or abroad, whether a secular priest or a member of an order—that was their ambition. For, to the Martins, a priest was a man exalted far above all men. Never in their home was any word uttered criticizing a priest, and all their children were brought up to hold them in the greatest reverence.

Céline declared of her father: "His respect for priests was so great that I never saw anything like it. I remember when I was a little child I imagined from what I heard that priests were like gods, for I was accustomed to have them placed above the common level." When Thérèse was taken on the pilgrimage to Rome, she had, as she says, never been in close touch with priests and she could not understand why one of the chief purposes of the Carmelites was to pray for them. She soon learned. Writing with great discretion, she says she lived for a month amidst many holy priests, but she discovered that, although the priestly dignity raises them above the angels, they are still weak and frail.

She gives no details, but the pilgrimage was largely made up of men and women of wealth and position, and it is not unlikely that Thérèse saw priests apparently too concerned with the ephemera of this world. Thérèse could have taken for her own the words of Pope John XXIII, for he, like her, sometimes found a great difference between priests as they were and priests as they should be. He said: "I see the purity of the priest's heart like a globe of purest crystal lit by the sun's radiance. My soul must be like a mirror to reflect the images of the angels, of Mary most holy, of Jesus Christ. If the mirror should cloud over, however slightly, then I deserve to be broken into pieces and flung onto the rubbish heap. O

God, I tremble when I think that not a few priests betray their sacred calling."

And Thérèse was deeply moved by the contrast between what she had been taught about priests at home and what she saw of some of them on her journey through Italy. She never forgot it. Much later, she would exclaim: "Alas! How many bad priests there are, priests who are not holy enough! Let us pray for them and suffer for them. Let us live for souls, let us be apostles, and above all, let us save the souls of priests, those souls which should be clearer than crystal." It is to Céline that she writes this, and it is not the only time she utters such an appeal: "Céline darling, I always say the same thing to you—let us pray for priests. Let us pray for them, let our lives be consecrated to them. Continually does Jesus make me feel that that is what He wants from us."

Céline has said that this desire to sanctify priests and, through them, to convert sinners was the real mainspring of Thérèse's life. She often said how greatly she regretted that she could never be a priest and, near death, remarked that God was going to take her at an age before she could have become a priest, even if her sex had not made it impossible.

She owed much to priests, two in particular. There was the Jesuit, Father Pichon, who was the spiritual director of the Martin sisters. Thérèse called him a director after St. Teresa's own heart, and she wrote him many letters. Most unhappily Father Pichon did not keep even one of them. Of her final letter to him, Thérèse said: "My whole soul was in it."

And in 1891, a Franciscan from Caen, Father Prou, gave a week's retreat at the Carmel. Thérèse says: "I felt inclined to say nothing about my deepest feelings, for I didn't know how to put them into words, but as soon as I entered the confessional my soul expanded. After saying only a word or two, I found myself completely understood. My soul was like a book the Father knew how to read better than I could. He launched me full sail upon that tide of confidence and love which had so strongly attracted me, but on which I had never dared set out. He told me that my faults did not cause God sorrow and declared: 'I stand in His place and, on His behalf, I tell you that He is very satisfied with you.' Oh! How happy I was to hear this! I'd never been told before that faults did not pain God. The priest's assurance filled me with joy and enabled me to bear my exile patiently."

Chapter 13

SUMMING UP

We are a little uneasy in the presence of sanctity. We see it so rarely, that one possessing it to so supreme a degree as St. Thérèse may seem at times a remote, hierarchical figure clad in the light of Paradise which dazzles us and hides her from us. It is an illusion. To read her own story should dispel it. She is, as she herself says, busy with souls until the End of Time. Her physical death, far from ending her commerce with her fellows, has widened it to cover the world. But now it is a one-sided commerce: she can do great things for us; there is nothing we can do for her. We can pray for her intercession and we can try to love God as she does, but she has no need of us. That does not make her remote. She is but a creature, "a grain of sand" alongside Our Lord, and yet we know that He, eternal and omnipotent, Creator of all that was, and is, and will be, is closer to us than the air we breathe and that it is impossible to comprehend the greatness of the love He bears us.

So how can St. Thérèse be distant when God is so near? Yet she is a saint and we know we are not, though each of us is called upon to be one. Saints though, unlike the pagan goddess, do not spring fully armed from the head of a god. They are not freaks and it is, I believe, consoling to see how much they owe to the people with whom they mixed during their life on earth, and how decisive the effect can be on them of a book, a picture, a chance encounter, a casual word—consoling, for we are reminded of their humanity, and sharply salutary, for we learn that everything we ourselves do or say, apart from

152

its effect on us, can strike a cord that will vibrate throughout eternity.

Let us look again for a moment at the little group who stand behind St. Thérèse, behind in the background, but picked out from the engulfing darkness of the past by the radiance which streams from her. We must not forget Rose Taillé, the buxom farmer's wife whose abundant breasts kept Thérèse alive; nor Pranzini, lecher, murderer and atheist, whose infamy would by now have vanished from our knowledge along with the police files in which it was recorded had not Thérèse and Céline won his redemption by their prayers and made him the "Good Thief" of our time; and the cripple, who, nameless but immortal for as long as Thérèse's words are read, rejected her alms and was remembered by her at her First Communion; the shadowy figure of the Abbé Arminjon; Isidore Guérin, her fiery, prosperous uncle; Victoire, the servant at Le Buissonnets; her father and mother; her sisters; Mother Marie de Gonzague; Father Pichon; the Franciscan Father Prou—could he ever have imagined that a retreat preached to a handful of Carmelite nuns would earn him the gratitude of millions of Christians then unborn? And there are the two missionaries with whom she corresponded; poor old Sister St. Pierre, in our imagination moving forever to the refectory along the cold, poorly lighted corridor of Carmel; Madame Papineau, her mother, and their cat, fixed for all time in their crowded, old-fashioned parlor; Father Delatroëtte thundering away at the folly of admitting a fifteen-year old child into Carmel; the Bishop of Bayeux, never for a moment realizing that, on a rainy October afternoon when he spoke kindly to a tearful girl, he stepped from the grey obscurity of his see.

They all played a part in the making of a saint. But St. Thérèse so greatly transcends her circle that, before leaving her, we must try to discover in what way she differed from, say, her parents and sisters, the people who had most influence on her. Shakespeare is unmistakable. Marlowe and Jonson, Webster and Ford enrich the literature of England, but a week spent reading them and Shakespeare is the quickest, surest way of appreciating the effortless superiority of Shakespeare. And the music of Bach, Mozart, and Beethoven has a final, unquestionable authority. In the world of secular genius, there is a handful of people whose quality of achievement impresses one as being wholly different in kind, not merely in degree, from that attained by those just below them, greatly talented though these latter are.

In the world of spiritual genius, St. Thérèse is one of a similar handful. Her parents were good, so good that their beatification and ultimate canonization are being sought, and using language loosely, her sisters were saintly women. But they cannot be compared with St. Thérèse. The Church has canonized her, so it may be said that fact lifts her high above her family, and knowing that she is a recognized saint, we shall, however dispassionate we try to be, inevitably give her attributes we should never have thought of assigning to her had she not been raised to the altars of the Church. But this is putting the cart before the horse. The qualities of Thérèse made her a saint; they did not become apparent only after Pius XI decreed that she is one.

There is, first of all, her precociousness. From the moment reason began to stir within her, she turned to God. She was as precocious spiritually as Mozart was musically. We know her so well that we have long ago ceased to wonder at her entry into Carmel when she was only fifteen, but it is an extraordinary fact that she was ready for Carmel at such an age.

Along with the phenomenally early development is her single-mindedness. As she herself has said, she never—and she meant this "never" to be taken literally—she never ceased thinking of God, never had a moment when she was not loving Him. She was interested in nothing else. Most young girls have hobbies. Thérèse had none. Most young girls have a few close friends. Thérèse had none outside her family. Her every thought, feeling and act pivoted around God. We have all probably known a fanatic, a person with a one-track mind, but because such a person is obsessed with matters like race, color, a philosophical theory, a system of politics, or something as trivial as a particular sport or diet, he is either very dull or very dangerous—as dull as the obsessive golfer or the man who believes the Pyramids hold the secret of the universe, or as deadly as Hitler. Equally as dull and dangerous are those who are obsessed by the wrong conception of God. They are the great heretics. But obsession with the true, the living God has a very different effect.

No Christian has ever found Thérèse dull. She becomes more fascinating with every year that passes. With only one purpose in life, with but one idea in her head and one emotion in her soul, she never gives any impression of one-sidedness, of any lack of balance, of any abnormality. She is rounded and complete. In modern jargon, she has a thoroughly integrated personality. We who read of her today are not the only ones to notice this. The nuns with whom she lived for more than nine years saw nothing abnormal about her. Her sisters knew towards the end of her life that she was a saint, but to be a saint is not an abnormality. It is a rare but eminently healthy condition.

The rest of the convent thought of her as a good and pleasant little thing. They were distressed if she were not at recreation, saying: "We shan't laugh to-day." It is, of course, impossible to be unbalanced if one's whole being is concentrated on God, for He is perfection; impossible to be dull, for He is the source of all vitality; impossible to have a narrow mind and shrunken personality, for He contains all things within Himself. To focus one's attention wholly on God is not a limiting, restricting act; it ensures that one achieves complete liberation—"you will," as Our Lord said, "have freedom in earnest." And that is the freedom St. Thérèse knew.

She was passionate. A great fire burned within her. Look again at some of the photographs of her and you can see, or sense, behind the still, calm face, the quiet gaze, the slightly smiling eyes, an intensity of feeling which, fully controlled though it be, is yet of a kind felt by only a handful of people in each generation. But this passion is not the wild, unbalanced emotion which stirred the romantic poets. St. Thérèse was not a romantic person. We must not be misled by the sentimentality of some of her language. Even when we have pared away the sugariness daubed on by Mother Agnès, there still remain phrases difficult to accept, but we must always remember that she was not a very well-educated girl and that her writing could not wholly escape the conventions that governed language in the circle within which she lived.

She herself was a realist. Her attitude was classical rather than romantic. What she said of herself was true: she had no illusions. That is why there is a hardness about her which some people find disconcerting. There is no soft center in Thérèse. "Hardness" nowadays is a word with bad moral undertones when applied to a person's nature. It should not be so. It all depends on what one is hard about, and to be hard is not at all the same thing as being callous. We know that Thérèse was patient, tender, and infinitely understanding in her relations with the other nuns of Carmel; she was hard, not because her sensibilities had atrophied, but because her will was single and undivided, because all her faculties were concentrated by her love of God as the diffused sunlight is by a burning-glass, and because both her instincts and her reason made her strip away from herself all that was irrelevant to her swift, sure flight to sanctity.

She had the sharp clarity of a diamond—and its hardness, its brilliance, and its purity. There may be some who prefer to see her as the "little flower" of her own story, feeling more comfortable to meet her in that guise. It is a very understandable attitude, but I would remind them that, in two of Our Lady's manifestations—at La Salette and at Fatima—she chose to appear as a figure "more brilliant than the sun," a figure as "bright as crystal with the sun streaming through it," and this dazzling radiance of the Mother of God put no barrier between her and the children with whom she spoke.

Still, St. Thérèse is a protean figure, in that we all find different things in her, hence the universality of her appeal. She receives homage from peasants and Popes. Truly, she is one of the wondrous works of God, and well may we end with her own words: "God always uses His creatures as the instruments with which He fashions souls."

If you have enjoyed this book, consider making your next selection from among the following . . .